LANDUSE PLANNING AND GEOMORPHOLOGY

LANDUSE PLANNING AND GEOMORPHOLOGY

A Study of Sawai Madhopur

KALYAN HIRONI

CONCEPT PUBLISHING COMPANY, NEW DELHI 110059

The Indian Council of Social Science Research gave the financial support towards the publication of this work. However, the responsibility for the contents of the book — facts, opinions, conclusions, etc. — is entirely that of the author and not of the ICSSR.

ICSSR Consultant : **PROF. S.L. KAYASTHA**

ISBN 81-7022-350-4

First Published 1991

Published and Printed by
Ashok Kumar Mittal
Concept Publishing Company
A/15-16, Commercial Block, Mohan Garden
NEW DELHI 110059 (India)

Lasertypeset by
Microtech Advance Printing Systems Pvt. Ltd.
H-13, Bali Nagar,
NEW DELHI 110015

ACKNOWLEDGEMENTS

I WISH to express my sincere sense of gratitude to my teacher and supervisor Dr. H.S. Sharma, Associate Professor in the Department of Geography, University of Rajasthan, Jaipur, whose indispensable guidance and sustained interests has enabled me to carry out the present work.

I am extremely grateful to Mrs. Kushal Singh, IAS, then Special Secretary Education, Rajasthan, Jaipur, for her inspiration and encouragement regarding this work. Similarly, I also offer my sincere gratitude to Professor J.M. Srivastava, Director of College Education and Professor Gyanendra Arora, Principal, Government College, Kota, who have been a constant source of encouragement.

Although, Professor Indra Pal and Professor N.L. Gupta have not directly involved actively in this study, yet they took pains to read the entire typescript and called my attention to errors of fact and infelicities of organisation, most of which I have corrected and modified.

I owe a debt of gratitude of Dr. (Mrs.) Laxmi Shukla, who has been kind enough to help me in various ways, Professor S.S. Dhabaria, Dr. N.S. Rathore and Dr. M.S. Nathawat of B.M. Birla Institute of Scientific Research, Jaipur, for their help in Remote Sensing Applications in the work.

I must express my gratitude to Mr. S.C. Agarwal, Senior Geologist at Kota, for his valuable suggestions regarding the geology of the area and Dr. Ratan Singh and Dr. Arora (ICAR, Kota) for their genuine interest and suggestions in landuse studies.

I looked to impose many friendly colleagues for advice and criticism; Dr. M.M. Jain, Dr. M.L. Sharma, and Mr. R.D. Gurjar, have each read and helped to eliminate many errors. I am grateful to them all.

I am again indebted to a number of people for their help and tolerance during the preparation of this thesis: my wife drew some of the diagrams and took more than a fair share of our domestic responsibilities allowing me to concentrate on this study; of my colleagues Mr. Basil Fernandez spent many hours critically reading and correcting on the whole text; and also received valued advice and comments from Mr. Sunil Bhargava regarding photography.

Last but not the least, I must thank Mrs. M.K. Singh, who typed this manuscript with full zeal; and Mr. Ram Avtar Sharma and Mr. P.R. Binda for doing their cartographic assistance.

30th November, 1987

KALYAN HIRONI

CONTENTS

LIST OF FIGURES

LIST OF TABLES

INTRODUCTION

GEOMORPHOLOGY IS the study of landforms, their origin and distribution. This science is entering into a new era of discovery and scientific excitement centred on expanding scales of concern in both time and space. The catalysts for this development include technological advances in Global Remote Sensing system, mathematical modelling and the dating of the geomorphic surfaces and processes. Even more important are new scientific questions centred on comparative planetary geomorphology, the interaction of tectonism with landscape, the dynamics of late Cenozoic climate changes, the influence of cataclysmic processes, the recognition of extremely ancient landforms, and the history of the world's hydrologic systems. These questions involve feedback relationship with allied sciences that have recently yielded profound development. The most significant scientific questions in Applied Geomorphology also have a global original context. Relevant concerns include the (i) accelerated erosion induced by deforestation, (ii) the paleogeomorphology of continental margin for petroleum exploration, (iii) the hydro-geomorphic consequences of carbon-dioxide warming, (iv) desertification, and (v) urban landscape metamorphosis.

The significance of geomorphological research is indicated by the fact that an international organisation of geomorphologists has been formed. The first international geomorphological conference, held at Manchester in 1985, was a major event in which specific emphasis was laid on the application of geomorphology in landuse planning. Out of 25 sessions, half of the sessions were concerned with applied geomorphology. Therefore, the utility of geomorphology in landuse planning is beyond doubt, although landuse pattern is the result of an interaction of the physical and socio-economic factors. The significance of the physical parameters cannot be overlooked.

India has taken a big stride in the field of geomorphology in the past two decades. Various universities, central and state government organisations such as the Geological Survey of India, the Survey of India, the National Atlas Organisation, the Soil and Landuse Survey, the central and state Ground Water Departments, the Space Application Research Organisation, Ahmedabad; the National Remote Sensing Agency, Hyderabad, have initiated serious geomorphological research according to their needs and requirements. A modest attempt has also been made to synthesis geomorphology land system. Landuse planning has been carried out in different parts of our country. Pioneer studies in this regard have been made by Ghose and Singh (1965), Vats and Singh (1983), of Central Research Arid Zone, Jodhpur, in Rajasthan, Vaidyanadhan R., Raghavswamy, V. in Coastal Andhra Pradesh, Sharma, H.S. (1979) in the Lower Chambal Valley, Rai, R.K. (1984) Landuse and soil erosion around Shillong. Similar studies were carried out by Klimoszewski (1985) for Karakov region of Poland, Cooke *et al.* (1974), Iyer and Srinivasan (1977), Subramanyam (1978) and by the Division of the Landuse Research, CSIRO of Australia.

Realising importance and application, the Remote Sensing Agency, Hyderabad, has sponsored major projects on district level wasteland mapping using TM data 1986 with 30 metres resolution at 1: 50,000 scale to Central Arid Research Institute and State Photo-interpretation Lab. under Science and Technology Department of Rajasthan. The present study of Geomorphology and landuse planning of Sawai Madhopur is a humble attempt in this direction.

THE STUDY AREA

The Sawai Madhopur district which has been chosen for the present study is located in the South-eastern part of Rajasthan between latitude 25°45′ north and 27°14′ north and longitude 75°59′ east and 77°23′ east. It is bound on the north by Alwar district, on the south by Kota and Bundi districts and the Chambal river forms a natural boundary in the east separating Madhya Pradesh, on the north-east by Bharatpur district and on the west and north-west by Tonk and Jaipur districts respectively (Fig. 1). The area of the district as reported by the Surveyor General of India is 4,070 sq miles or 10.543.6 sq km. The district is composed of eleven tahsils. Physiographically, a major part of the district is covered by the thick alluvium deposited by the Banas, the Gambhiri, the Morel and the Chambal systems. The southern part of the district is occupied by the Vindhayans and the quartzites of the Aravalli system. These are separated from the main expanse of the

Vindhyan by the Chambal Valley and its ravines. A number of isolated hills, mostly occupied by the rocks of the older metamorphics, are scattered in the alluvial tract. Climatically, it falls under the semi-arid climate with an average annual rainfall of 685.8 millimetres and the maximum temperature goes up to about 47°C in June.

FIG. 1

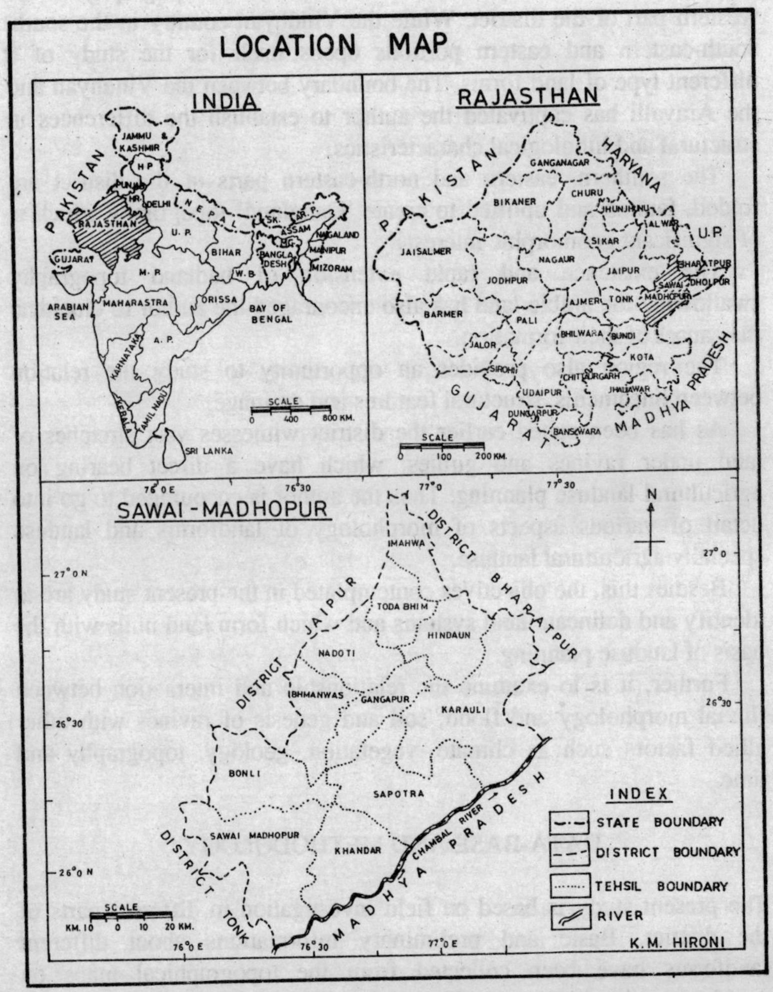

CHOICE AND OBJECTIVES OF THE STUDY

The conspicuous location of Sawai Madhopur district itself is of great geomorphic significance. The area lies between the pre-Aravalli and the Vindhyan Super Groups which has given rise to a variety of landforms. The scattered structural hills (of Aravalli Super Group) on the alluvial plains composed of highly metamorphosed rocks present an opportunity to study the characteristics of the topography of the western part of the district. While the Vindhyan country in the south, south-eastern and eastern portions opens itself for the study of a different type of land forms. The boundary between the Vindhyan and the Aravalli has captivated the author to establish the differences in structural and lithological characteristics.

The southern, eastern and north-eastern parts of the district are folded, faulted and uplifted to create 'Dangland' topography which is of significant geomorphic interest.

The existence and rapid extension of badland topography swallowing the arable land has also encouraged the author to elucidate the causes of their formation.

The region also provides an opportunity to study the relation between lineaments, structural features and drainage.

As has been stated earlier the district witnesses vast stretches of land under ravines and gullies, which have a direct bearing on agricultural landuse planning. Thus the author is encouraged to go into detail of various aspects of morphology of landforms and landuse specially agricultural landuse.

Besdies this, the objectives contemplated in the present study are to identify and delineate land systems and which form land units with the basis of landuse planning.

Further, it is to examine the relationship and interaction between fluvial morphology and flood, soil and genesis of ravines with other allied factors such as climate, vegetation, geology, topography and time.

DATA-BASE AND METHODOLOGY

The present study is based on field investigation in different parts of the district. Basic and preliminary informations about different landforms have been collected from the topographical maps on 1: 50,000, viz. 54 B/4, 7, 8, 9, 11, 14, 15 and 54 C/8 and 9 and

1: 250,000 viz., 54A, B, C, E, and F. After collecting the preliminary informations detailed field traverses were made to verify the corresponding features on the ground. Special attention was paid during fieldwork on different forms of slopes, processes operating on different forms, slope elements, nature of different morphological units and their associations with different type of landuse categories. Multispectral landsat and TM 2, 3, 4, 1986 data have also been used to prepare a geomorphological map of the district on 1: 250,000 scale.

The basic morphometric attribute, like drainage frequency, drainage density, slope, analysis, altimetric frequency histogram, serial profiles, projected and superimposed profiles, long and cross profiles of rivers have been enumerated. The analysis of soil samples were done at the Soil Research Institutes, Durgapura, Jaipur, and climatic data were collected from the Indian Meteorological Department, Jaipur, and Department of Hydrology, Government of Rajasthan, Jaipur.

The boundaries of different landforms units were delimited and salient erosional and depositional geomorphic features of each unit were discussed. The landuse patterns under different landforms were also interpreted and mapped and were also compared with the corresponding landuse patterns in the field. The geomorphic and landuse maps were superimposed on each other and a map showing the morpho-landuse pattern was prepared. Landuse data of eleven tahsils were collected and decadal change have been worked out.

CHAPTERISATION SCHEME

The work has been divided into nine chapters.

The first chapter is devoted to a detail geological description and climatic base. The first section deals with geological history and rock formation in chronological order. The structural features like the Great Boundary Fault, lineaments, joints and faults have been dealt with. The second section of this chapter represents the study of climatic conditions of the district. The area has extremes of temperatures and rainfall with severe experiences of floods. Different seasons in the district, namely, pre-monsoon, monsoon, post-monsoon and winters have been discussed thoroughly. Rainfall intensity and distribution have also been included.

The second chapter includes the properties of soils. A detail account of soil types, texture, chemical analysis and soil fertility status have been taken in the view. The factors affecting soil genesis e.g.

climate, parent material, topography, vegetation and time have been also fully elucidated. A detail soil map is also given compiled.

The third chapter touches a vital aspect of fluvial morphology of the Chambal, the Banas, the Gambhir and the Morel and their tributaries. The long and cross profiles of all main rivers have been analysed. Various drainage patterns, drainage frequency and drainage density are also analysed in relation to their controlling factors.

The fourth chapter deals with the Flood Morphology. After looking into flood incidents in the district, the flood of 1981 has been discussed in detail. Sawai Madhopur is predominantly a flood prone district. The various causes and conditions of flood like climatic factors; discharge and run-off, topographical factors, geological factors, palaeo-drainage and vegetation have been analysed.

The fifth chapter deals with the morphology of ravines and gullies. It also touches the four main ravine areas of the district namely, the Gambhir-Panchai, Manchi ravine area, the Banas-Chambal Confluence, the Morel-Banas and the scattered ravined areas. Simultaneously, classification, factors of ravine erosion, and shape and size are also given in detail.

In the sixth chapter an attempt has been made to delimit geomorphic regions of Sawai Madhopur district. Geomorphic properties of each region and the dominating landforms and features within these units have been described.

The seventh chapter presents the existing landuse pattern with variation of ten years. The changing picture of landuse has been depicted. Landuse table has been discussed under the heads of forest, land put to non-agricultural use, barren and uncultivable land, other uncultivable land excluding fallowland, culturable waste, fallowland, net area sown and double cropped area.

Chapter eight is an essence of the work, e.g. geomorphology and landuse planning in which application of slope map in landuse has been discussed. In the last suggested landuse plan for the district has been discussed. A strategy has also been worked out as a suggestive measure for improving the quality of landuse with reference to the geomorphology of the region. A number of suggestions have been made for providing a better understanding of the geology, soils, the fluvial morphology, the flood morphology and methods of abatement and the ravine reclamation of the region.

The ninth chapter presents the summery of the work and landuse planning.

1

GEOLOGY AND CLIMATE

GEOLOGY

IN THE geomorphological study of a particular region the knowledge of its geology is most essential. The genesis of the present day landscape has largely to be sought in the geology of the region.

Sawai Madhopur district is characterised by the northern extension of the Vindhyan plateau covering the south-eastern part of the district. The geology of the district is bewildering in complexity. The terrain comprises pre-Cambrian metamorphic, igneous and sedimentary rocks belonging to pre-Aravallis and Vindhyan. Alluvium soil is primarily confined to the vicinity of the Banas river covering the area between the Great Boundary Fault and the Lalsot hill ranges, which form the western boundary of the district.

The district under study is tectonically the north-western part of the Indian table land. It has been pointed out by geomorphologists and geologists that this part of the Indian table land has been unaffected by any tectonic movement of organic nature, except some side effects of various phases of the Himalayan Orogeny. In the Cretaceous period with the rejuvenation of the Aravallis, the rocks of the region have been folded and faulted. These activities brought the older pre-Aravalli meta-sediments in juxtaposition to the sedimentaries of the Vindhyans.

The pre-Aravalli rocks are mainly banded hematic-jasper quartzites and limestone. They occur between Lalsot and Bayana dolerites. The Delhi Super Group comprises conglomerates, quartzites and meta-volcanic rocks of the Alwar group. The Vindhyan Super Group as represented by the Kaimur, Rewa and Bhandar groups, consists mainly of various type of shales, sandstones and limestones. These rocks occupy the south-eastern part of the district and are separated from the older rocks by a major reverse fault, the great Boundary Fault, trending north-east to south-west. Due to amalgamation of such heterogeneous features within a single region, Sawai Madhopur has been aptly called the 'Varitable Museum of Rajasthan Geology'.

Previous Work on Geology

Though the first well recognised study of the geology of Sawai Madhopur district was carried out about 70 years ago, the comprehensive work intended to classify the rocks in chronological order was made in 1917 by Heron, A.M. This pioneer effort was succeeded by a few publications by Pascoe, E.C.(1953 and 1959), Ghose, P.K. (1952), Roy, B.C. (1972), Banerjee, A.K. (1976), Balmiki Prasad (1984), Iqbaluddin (1976).

During the past two decades a large part of Rajasthan has been re-mapped on the basis of aerial photographs. It has shed a new light on the stratigraphy of the State. Therefore, the modified stratigraphic sequence of the district is given in Table 1.1.

TABLE 1.1: Geological Formation in Sawai Madhopur District

Sl. No.	Period	Age (m.y.)	Group	Formations	Rock type
1.	Quaternary	1	Recent	Recent to sub-recent	Sand, alluvium, etc.
2.	Lower Palae-ozoic to upper Proterozoic	1400-400	Vindhyan Super Group	Bhandar group	Sandstone, limestone
				Rewa group	Shales and sandstone
				Kaimur group	Sandstone, conglome-rate
				Semri group	Limestone, sandstone and shale
3.	Proterozoic	1400-2500	Delhi Super Group	Alwar group	Quartzites, conglome-rates and schists
		ca 2000 ma	Aravalli Super Group	Gwalior group	Dolerites, shales and quartzites, Hematite shales
4.	Archaen	3600	—	Pre-Aravalli group	Schists, gneisses, phyllites, marbles and quartzites

The geological description of the district (Fig. 1.1) is based on the information collected from the Memoirs and Records of the Geological Survey of India.

FIG. 1.1

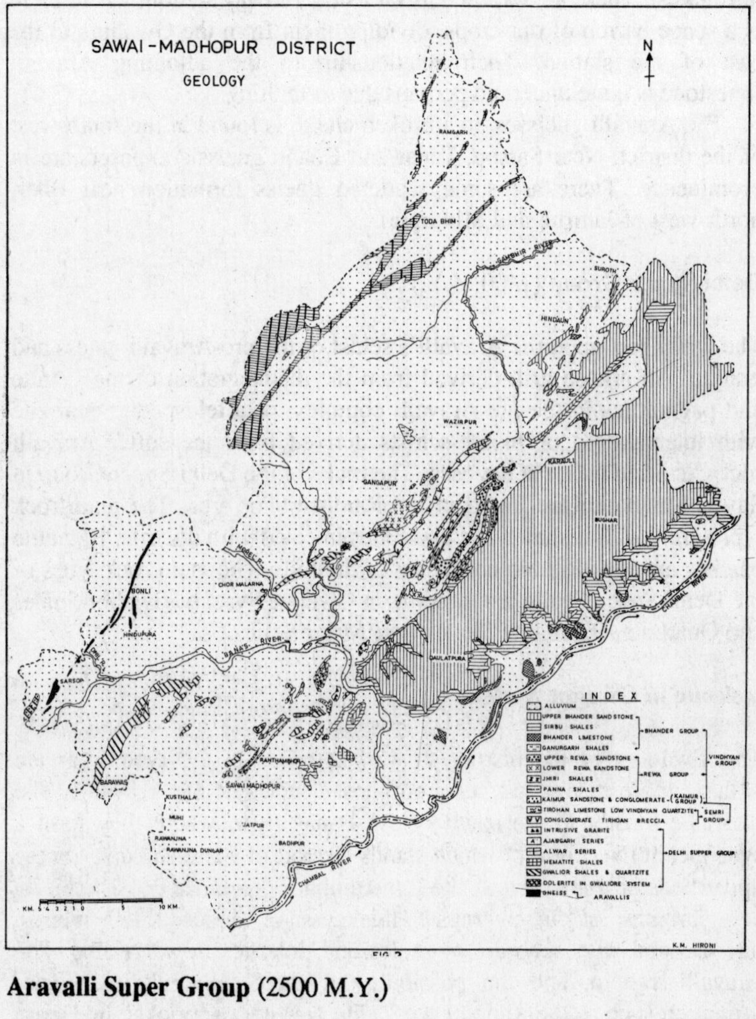

Aravalli Super Group (2500 M.Y.)

The rocks of this system are of great thickness, dominantly argillaceous in composition and progressively becoming more metamorphosed. The only rocks which can be placed with certainty in the Aravalli system occur to the west of Chouth-ka-Barwara (26°3′, 76°13′), a series of actinolitic and ferruginous quartz veined crystalline limestone and amphibolites, very imperfectly seen in water courses between here and the Banas river and dipping at 15°-16° to the north-west. These are exposed as far as the railway station, where there is a space barren of out-crops, dividing them from the Gwaliors to the east of the station. Their relationship to the adjoining Aravalli limestone is quite uncertain perhaps due to faulting.

The Aravalli gneisses, in a broken chain, is found in the south-west of the district. Near Sarsop, Tapar and Boanli gneissic exposers are in prominence. There are some scattered gneiss formation near Bher, north-west of Jamruli and Mittarpuri.

Delhi Super Group (1400 M.Y.)

The Delhi rest upon the Aravalli's schist or the pre-Aravalli gniess and granite. An arkose grit, derived from the disintegration of the granite and pagmatites in the pre-Aravalli complex, or a feldspathic quartzite with intercalation of biotite-schists derived from the softer Aravalli rocks, is often found at the base. The rocks of the Delhi Super Group in Sawai Madhopur are found in the Ranthambhor area. The main rock types are Gwalior shales and quartzites injected with dolerite. Hamatite patches are found in the north-east of the hills. The main rock types of the Delhi Super Group are: dolerite in Gwalior System, Gwalior Shales and Quartzite, Haematite Shales, and Alwar Series.

Dolerite in Gwalior System

The Gwaliors of the district as well as those of the type areas are nothing more than a less metamorphosed facies of the Aravallis. The rocks lie mostly to the south of the Banas river, where they form a syncline, at the centre of which stands the fort of Ranthambhor. On the upper beds of this syncline, the Ranthambhor quartzites consist chiefly of quartzites of an aggregate thickness of about 1,060 metres, inter-bedded with subordinate shales and dolerites flows or sills. The Aravalli system, and the possibility of their belonging to a later formation such as the Railo or the Delhi, was not overlooked by Heron (1927). The interbedded shales and dolerites are described as of Gwalior type. Dolerite out crops are seen in Khalupura, Lodhipur and Ram Singhpura in Sawai Madhopur and Kachida Kalan, Lakkarda and Berda in Khandar Tahsil.

Gwalior Shales and Quartzites

The quartzites are, in general, pink or reddish and are evenly coloured without mottling or banding. They are more compact and quartzitic than Vindhyan. A peculiar type of quartzite is present here in the Ranthambhor. It is pink to dark-reddish-purple, fine textured, crystalline, unbedded and with irregular splintery jointing. Gwalior shale and quartzites hill at Kushtala is a typical example of this kind.

Shales and Slates

The shales also are rather distinctive. They are generally much less friable and fissile than the typical Vindhyan shales. They are most compact into thicker layers, harder and traversed by rectangular prismatic jointing. Above Dhurmurmal-ka-Darwaza, they consist of thin dull-red hematite shally beds alternating with white cherty or porcellanic bands and the normal black, red and grey shales. In the south-west of the district the scattered exposers like in Bhagawatgarh (26°8′, 76°18′). These are a monotonous stretches of reddish-brown and purple slates, near schists, with a well developed cleavage in the north-east to south-west direction.

Haematite Shales

There is no clear haematite exposure as quartzites and shales. But in the south-east of the Banas river near Lakkarda and Berda a big patch of haematite has been identified, shown in the map (Fig. 1.1). Another outcrops along the line of strike at Hindaun, are somewhat peculiar. They consist of layers of black, siliceous haematite alternating with white chert or bright-red jesper.

Alwar Series

The Alwar series extend along the district boundary line of Jaipur with Sawai Madhopur. Two off-shoots are clearly visible, one from Bamanwas to Mahuwa tehsil and the other goes towards the north-east direction up to Tilchiri (Mahuwa). The Alwar series is well developed in the region and rests uncomformably on the pre-Aravalli gneiss. The quartzites as well as the arkose grits are also seen. The arkose, grits and quartzites, which represent the base beds, rest upon gneiss or the gneissic complex, with an erosion unconformity. Hacket (1881) carries the Gwaliors or, rather what he terms 'The Alwar Quartzite' for about 19 km further to the north-east of the Banas river. He writes as follows: "On the other side of the fault, the Alwar quartzite dips at high angle to the north-east resting upon the quartzite in a thickband of limestone with a siliceous breccia above it, above that, sandstone, with two alternation of shales and sandstones, to the top of the section."

VINDHYAN SUPER GROUP

The Delhis are succeeded by the Vindhyan after a time interval marked by earth movements and erosion. The name Vindhyan Super Group, after the Vindhyan mountains, in a large basin cover over 1,04,000 sq km of Central India. Another 78,000 sq km of sediments lie concealed below the lava of the Deccan trap.

In the eastern Rajasthan the entire Vindhyan succession is well developed. They were deposited in a large basin extending from Karauli and Dholpur to the north-east. The north-eastern and south-western outcrops are connected by narrow, disconnected patches extending from Sawai Madhopur to Bundi. In the district the distribution of Vindhyan Super Group is well developed, depicted in (Fig. 1.2). From the north of the Banas near Haroti towards the north-east up to the Jamura the Upper Bhandar Sandstone covers a big portion. In the same direction the eastern margin of the Bhandar Sandstone is occupied with Sirbu Shales and Bhandar Limestone along the Chambal river. Bichpuri, Karanpur, Arora, Chandeli and Manakhur are the chief exposers of Sirbu shales. While Barel, Tigir, Rodhain and Mandrael are the representatives of Bhandar limestones. The western margins of Bhandar sandstone are covered with the upper and lower Rewa sandstone, Jhiri and Panna shales and conglomerates, quartzites and Tirhon breccia of Kaimur and Semri groups respectively. The main sub-divisions of the Vindhyan of Sawai Madhopur are: Semri Group, Kaimur Group, Rewa Group, and Bhandar Group.

In the south-western part of the Vindhyan basin in eastern Rajasthan, the formation have reached a maximum thickness of 450 metres; the lower and upper divisions being 900 metres and 360 metres, respectively. The Vindhyans have been affected by over thrust from the west, resulting in a Great Boundary Fault of about 805 km length with throw of some 500 metres. This has brought the undisturbed upper Vindhyans against the highly folded Aravallis.

FIG. 1.2

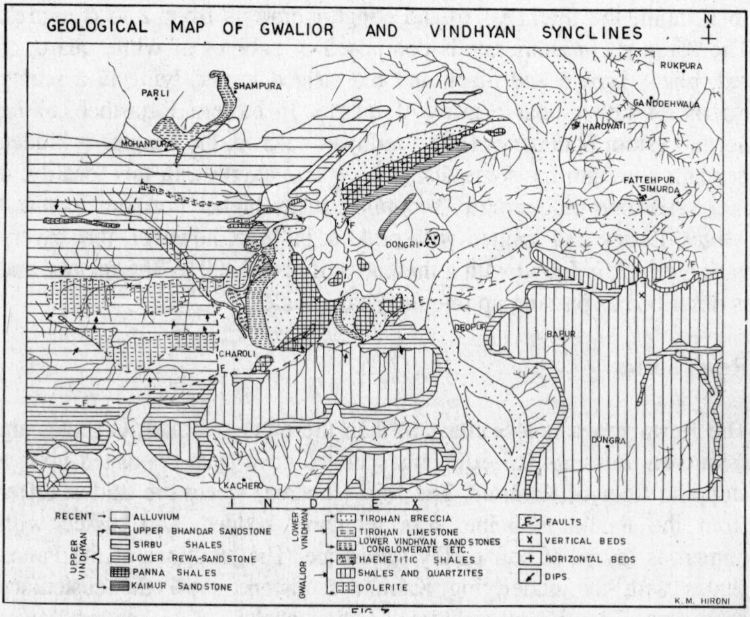

Semri Group (1400 M.Y.)

Tirhon Limestone

The Tirhon limestone is exposed at intervals only dipping at low angles below the breccia. The maximum thickness exposed does not exceed 9 or 12 metres. The rocks dolomitised and are identical in appearance with the limestone at Tirhon. Interbedded with shale and quartzites and at one place a band of silicified dolite have been observed.

Tirhon Breccia

The Tirhon breccia varies from a crypto-crystallive silicious matrix containing sharply angular fragments of all sizes of pure white chert. The breccia is unstratified; its thickness is difficult to estimate but it is not likely to exceed 60 metres. There is clear field-evidence that the breccia is autoclastic in origin.

Kaimur Series (900 M.Y.)

In Karauli, the thickness of the conglomerate is from 2 to 6 metres. The Kaimur conglomerate is composed of pebbles of white quartz of red, black, brown and black and red striped jesper, lying in a scanty matrix of rather coarse grins of quartz. In eastern Rajasthan, along north-western boundary of the Vindhyan outcrop, the Kaimur is hidden beneath alluvium for some distance. Where exposed in this locality, it is a sandstone or quartzite, becoming in its higher horizon finer and whiter, flaggy and spotted with pink. It is, here, however, that a very variable rock is found with a thickness of about 300 to 365 metres, and is described as passing up into the Panna shales.

Rewa Series

The Rewa series is less constant than the other two and its stages are frequently missing: its sediments seem to have been deposited upon a slopping floor of Kaimurs. The Jhiri (Jheeree) shales are said to differ from the Panna is being, less regularly bedded, and mixed with numerous layers of soft earthy sandstone. The junctions of the Panna shales with the underlying Kaimur sandstone show the customary sharpness. The thickness here is Panna shales — 45 metres; lower Rewah sandstone — 75 metres and the Jhiri shales; giving a total of 275-300 metres.

The distribution of the Rewah series is mostly in the west of the Aravalli hills and the east of the railway line, mostly on slopy areas near Samakanpur, Baroli, Barthua and Khadakpur.

Bhandar Series

The distribution of the upper Bhandar sandstone and Sirbu shales is prominent in the hilly tract of Sawai Madhopur, Khandar and Karauli. Sandstone is found on the higher areas. It follows Sirbu shales downward. The Bhandar limestone extends along the west of the Chambal river.

In eastern Rajasthan, the bright-red and yellow Ganurgarh shales, with 45-75 metres thickness, resting on the upper Rewah sandstone, pass up into the Bhandar limestone. The Bhandar limestone is the most variable rock of the series. In Karauli, its thickness is 75 metres. This limestone is typically gray-blue but sometimes pink or purple in colour.

Sirbu shales in Karauli are 150-180 metres thick. All the cliffs rising from the low ravine country near the Chambal and known as the Kherar, are composed of these shales, dark-red and olive in colour.

In the region the upper Bhandar the sandstone stage is 150-180 metres thick and covers the surface of the plateau, a part of which — locally known as the 'Dang' has been separated from the main portion by the Chambal river flowing from the south-west to the north-east. From the bold scarp overlooking the river there is a very gentle decline of the Dang surface north-westward, towards the Karauli city.

Alluvium

The largest area of the district is covered by recent and sub-recent deposits, consisting mainly of alluvium. The source of parent material of this alluvium has been the Aravallis and Vindhyan systems. This recent terrain that compose the vast alluvial basins is environmentally vulnerable, being intrinsically in a state of dynamic equilibrium between the natural forces and the soil water system with continuing modifications by human agencies in the form of agriculture and extensive urban or industrial settlements.

The alluvium of this region is fairly rich in nitrogen, potash and humus and covers wide-pread areas in the northern, north-western, western and south-western portions of the district. The Banas, the Morel, the Gambhir and the Banganga have been bringing an enormous quantity of water, silt and sediments during the rainy season and have been depositing it into the lower courses. These alluvial plains are interrupted by scattered patches of ridges of different rock types. The alluvium consists mainly of coarse to fine sand, sand loam, *kankar* and silt with occasional clay bands.

Structural Features

The Great Boundary Fault

The major dislocation marking the eastern fringe of the Aravalli has the length of 805 km and throw of 1,500 metres. It has played a dominant role in the architecture of the Vindhyan with the Aravallis. The dislocation called the Great Boundary Fault, comprises of a narrow linear zone of fractures. Its northern extremity is seen near

Fatehpur Sikri and its southern end can be observed at Pratapgarh.

In the district at Ranthambhor this fault is distinct where it passes from Sherpur up to the ravines. Further more in Sapotra tahsil it converts into two parallel faults in south-west to north-east direction. Both run through the Dangland in Karauli tahsil and leave the district near Behrda and Dhamonia Khoh. Besides this there are six transverse faults which are perpendicular to the Great Boundary Fault. These transverse faults control the direction and flow of the streams, like Karsil in Sapotra, Nahro in Karauli and Jagar in Hindaun which flow through the transverse faults. One separate fault line runs along the Chambal river.

There is no field evidence as to the nature of the fault in terms of its being a normal or reversed fault. If it is a normal fault then the throw and hade are to the south-east. It was considered, however, by Hacket (1881) and Coulson (1927) that the thrust was from the north-west, and that the Gwaliors have risen relatively to the Vindhyans. Thus, the fault is treated as Reversed Fault.

Folds and Lineament Structure

The important structural elements of the spear zone are linear structures and folds. Lineaments are only visible in the Dangland. It covers Sapotra and Karauli tahsils. In north-east of Karauli the lineament and faults are intermingled and present classic scene of structural importance.

Another significant structural feature of the district is the arrangement and nature of folds. Gently dipping synclines and anticlines are common. South of the Dangland, the faulting is less important and the Vindhyans have been folded. Ranthambhor is a good example of syncline. The northern boundary of this syncline is remarkably regular, following the folding of the Bhandar and Rewa sandstones and limestones. The Vindhyan rocks were tilted, deformed and folded during Cretaceous period.

Climate

Climate is an important factor in modifying the topography of a region. It has been established that the distinctive assemblage of geomorphic processes and landforms occur in an area with specific climates. Similarly, climatic accidents and temporal changes could occur in any given area, resulting in the formation of polygenetic landforms. For example, vast fields of mobile sand ridges are found only in the tropical arid lands. Coastal foredunes, the ridges of sand found in many places directly inland from beaches, are not represented well in the humid tropics as in the mid-latitude lands.

Sawai Madhopur district enjoys a semi-arid to sub-humid climate and lies at the junction between the eastern fringe of the Aravalli mountain and the north-western lobe of the Vindhyan basin of India. It gets rainfall partly by the monsoon winds of the Bay of Bengal and partly by the Arabian sea branch.

According to Koppen's (1954) classification the area falls into 'Bsh' type of climate. It's connotations are as under:

B stands for dry climates
s for dry season in summers of the respective hemisphere, and
h means dry and hot. Mean annual temperature over 18.0°C.

Sawai Madhopur has 15 rain gauge stations out of which 9 are in working order, established by the Department of Hydrology, Government of Rajasthan, Jaipur. The rain gauge stations record only rainfall observations. As far as analysis of temperature is concerned, there is not a single meteorological observatory in the district. Therefore, temperature and evaporation, atmospheric pressure, wind velocity and direction data utilised are that of Kota, Dholpur and Tonk, which are on the peripheries of the district. Only a hydrological station, by the Irrigation Department, has been installed at Shri Mahaveerji, which also records temperature and other river gauging.

Seasons

The district has been divided into four major seasons on the basis of standard meteorological conditions:

Pre-monsoon (March, April and May)
Monsoon (June, July, August and September)
Post-monsoon (October, November and December)
Winter (January and February).

It is an established fact that the dividing line between the two seasons is purely hypothetical since a month can be evolved into the other season at different times.

Pre-monsoon (March, April and May)

In March with the northward movement of the sun the temperature rises rapidly. Atmospheric pressure falls in sympathy over the heated land, but the sub-tropical anti-cyclonic cell persist. The jet stream which is a permanent feature gradually shifts northwards and migrates to a high level (220 mbs). The isobars have a flat pressure distribution due to the increased heating of the land. The pressure gradient is not strong enough and the isobaric pressure gradient is from the coast towards the diffused low on the Indian sub-continent. And it prevails more or less in the same pattern during the month of May.

In April and half of May, as the air is now drier in these months, dust storms are the maximum due to the western disturbances. The upper air inversions occur in May due to which the air is dust laden and for many days the sky is hazy.

The temperature conditions during pre-monsoon, in the district, show an increasing trend. At Sawai Madhopur the average maximum and minimum temperatures in March are 30.0°C and 13.5°C, in April 36.5°C and 19.5°C and in May 44.5°C and 26°C respectively. The temperature conditions are shown in the Temperature Chart (Fig. 1.3) and Appendix I. The temperature of June is slightly higher than May. Sometimes these temperatures reach up to 47°C. This steady rise in temperature results into a decrease in pressure, subsequently leading to hot dry weather. During the month of March, April and May, a rise of 10°C temperature is noted. In the month of March, the sky is usually clear with hardly 3 to 4 Octas of cumulus clouds, which is observed when troughs of low pressure cross from the west to the east. Normal rainfall during this period is generally absent, being only 10 to 15 millimetres and sometimes accompanied by the thunderstorms.

The relative humidity is also low due to little rainfall in pre-monsoon season. It is 58 per cent in March, 33 per cent in April and 30 per cent in May at Sawai Madhopur.

The surface wind is light and calm during the night. The winds are generally light to moderate with some strengthening in force in the summer. In this season, the direction of the winds is between south-west and north-west.

Monsoon (June, July, August and September)

In the beginning of June the features of the hot season just described are intensified, and the heat and drought become unbearable in the Gangetic plain. The jet stream which had already started migrating northwards from April, has now moved north of 30°N latitude where its velocity is considerably weakened and the south-west monsoon sets in. The low is very intense in June, July and August and weakens in September. The air is saturated with vapour and thick masses of clouds cover the sky and cause heavy rain and thunder. The arrival of monsoon over the eastern Rajasthan is normally by the end of June, when the whole area is engulfed with equatorial maritime airmass.

FIG 1.3

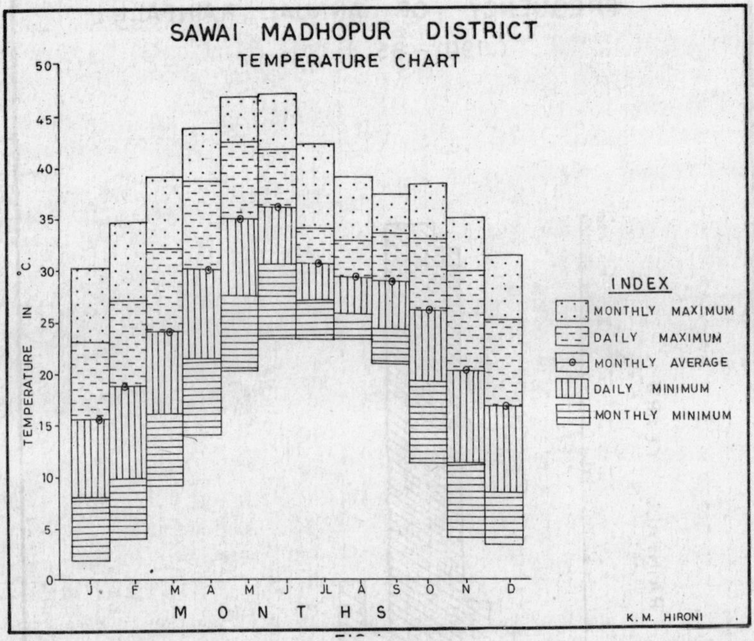

The major portion of the rain that falls in the area is due to monsoon depressions which form at the head of Bay. These depressions cross the Indian sub-continent and merge with the seasonal low. The average number of these lows is about one per week in the month of July and lessens in September. The rainfall is usually associated with these lows and it does not exceed five centimetres in 48 hours. It has been observed that between July and August, 80 per cent of the annual rainfall is received in this region, with August as the month with the heaviest rainfall. The areas lying in the east, south-east and the north (Sawai Madhopur, Karauli, Khandar and Hindaun tehsils) receive more rainfall which is generally orographic in character. During the rainy months the amount of surface runoff, sediments load and the magnitude of fluvial erosion are the highest. The amount of rainfall shows considerable variation from year to year which is evident from Appendix II. Similarly the frequency of rainfall during 1901 to 1985 is illustrated by Fig. 1.4 and the Table 1.2.

FIG. 1.4

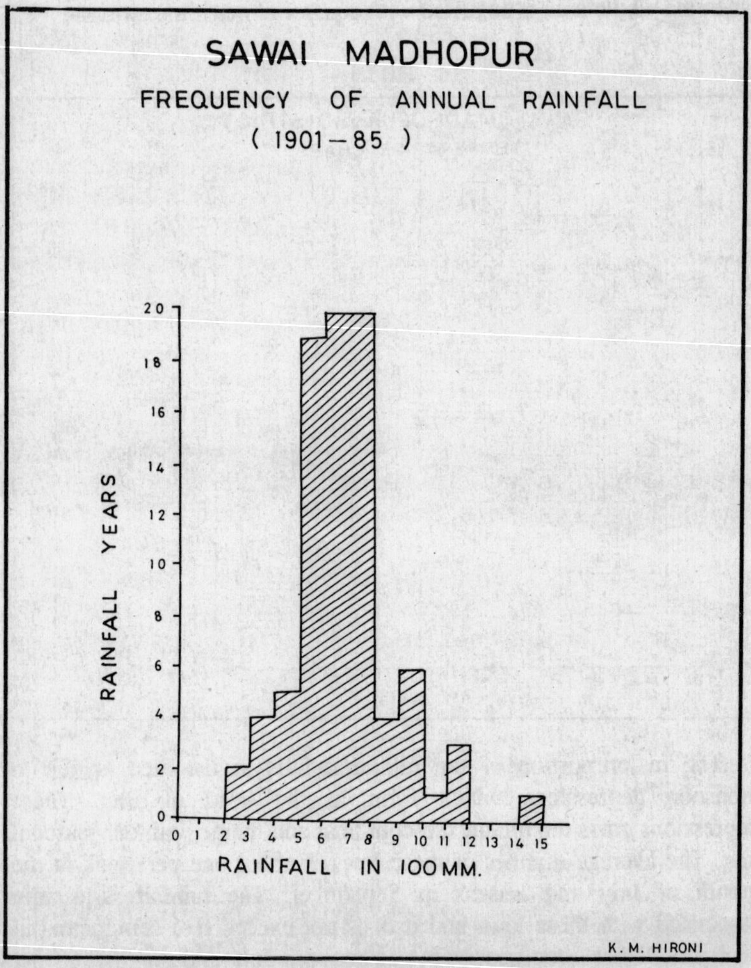

TABLE 1.2: Frequency of Rainfall (1901-1985)

Range in mm	Frequency of occurrence	Range in mm	Frequency of occurrence
201-300	2	901-1000	1
301-400	4	1001-1100	0
401-500	4	1101-1200	3
501-600	19	1201-1300	0
601-700	18	1301-1400	0
701-800	20	1401-1500	1
801-900	5		

The mean monthly rainfall during the rainy months i.e. March, April, May and June in Sawai Madhopur is 78.00, 336.00, 306.00 and 124.00 millimetres, respectively. The heaviest rainfall of 505 millimetres, in 24 hours, was recorded in Bamanwas (19 July, 1981). In the four months of the monsoon Khandar receives average rainfall 86.00, 227.00, 231.4, 129.0; Gangapur 52.1, 227.0, 223.3, 101.0; Hindaun 49.0, 219.5, 227.0, 107.0 and Karauli 53.0, 241.3, 244.0, 108.0 millimetres, respectively. Figure 1.5 shows the normal rainfall in the district (Appendix III).

There is hardly any rainfall worth mentioning seen in other months except in the monsoon period. The stations mentioned above are mainly located in the hilly regions, except Gangapur. During these months winds strike from the westerly and south-westerly directions and provide rain in the southern and western slopes of the hills of the district. The rainfall intensity of the four months of the monsoon period at these stations, varies from 18.94, 24.55, 18.10 and 19.99 millimetres respectively.

The value of relative humidity is the highest in this season due to the heavy rainfall and the presence of abundant moisture in the atmosphere. Its value at Sawai Madhopur is 54 per cent, 80 per cent, 84 per cent and 75 per cent respectively, during the monsoon months.

During the monsoon the moisture is the highest in the atmosphere with the result evaporation is minimum. June, July, August and September represent 550, 450, 450 and 350 millimetres evaporation in Sawai Madhopur.

The maximum and the minimum values of temperature recorded at Sawai Madhopur in the months of June, July, August and September of monsoon are 36.5°C and 21.5°C; 39.9°C and 21.0°C; 28.5°C and 24.5°C; 26.5°C and 24.5°C, respectively. The mean monthly temperatures recorded for June, July, August and September, at the stations, are 36.0°C, 30.2°C, 28.7°C and 28.2°C respectively. The temperature chart (Fig. 1.3) reveals the decreasing temperature conditions during these months. The diminishing temperatures bring about high pressure over the area. During the aforesaid four months the sky is usually covered with cumulus and alto-cumulus clouds. July and August have the maximum cloud cover of 6.0 and 6.1 octas in the district.

FIG 1.5

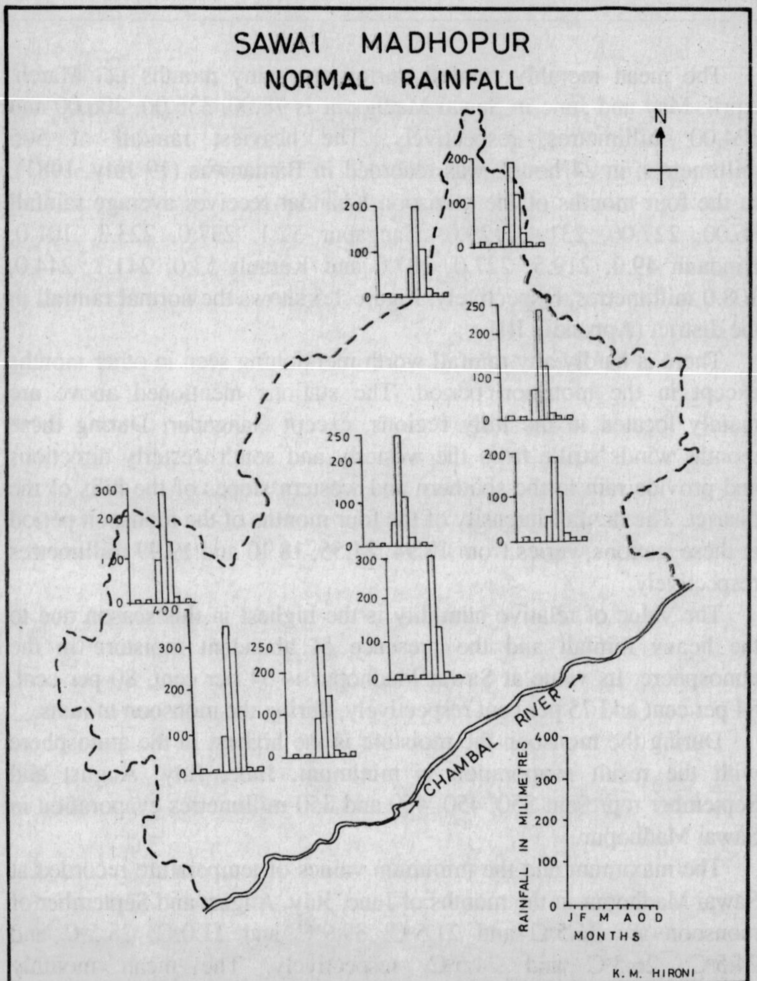

In a normal year the south-west monsoon continues till the first week of September. Then, as a result of the falling temperature, the atmospheric pressure increases in the north of the plains, and the monsoonal currents begin to loose strength and are no longer able to reach the area. The rainfall is meagre in the months of October and November. For Sawai Madhopur tehsil it is only 21.5 and 2.6 millimetres, whereas Khandar, Karauli and Hindaun, have recorded 11.00 and 1.5; 16.0 and 4.0; 14.4 and 4.2 millimetres rainfall respectively (Appendix III). By the middle of September the monsoon leaves the district. Again a short spell of hot season starts which may continue up to the middle of October. In the beginning of October the pressure is fairly uniform and the tendency of isobars shows high pressure.

Post-Monsoon Season (October, November and December)

The withdrawal of the south-west monsoon denotes the retreat of the rain-bearing south-west winds. In this retreating period the prevailing local winds dominate the circulatory conditions and affect the south-west monsoon inversely. During this period, i.e. October November and December, there is hardly any rainfall, due to anti-cyclonic conditions prevailing on the area. The period is witnessed with clear skies, the sun shines again, and the temperature rises for a few weeks before falling to its winter minimum. The relation of the temperature and the rainfall is clear from the climatic chart (Fig. 1.6).

Jet streams make their appearance in late October and about 200 mbs (12 km) and as the season advances it comes as low as 300 mbs.

It is noticed that appreciable rain falls in late November due to the appearance of the western disturbances over the district. The rainfall is sharp and of a short duration, sometimes accompanied by hail due to the low freezing level. Heavy rains only occur when an occluded front is formed. Inversions are common feature during this period. Hence, mist prevails in the morning. Due to lesser rains the relative humidity is also less. Its values are 64 per cent, 68 per cent and 72 per cent in the three post-monsoon months.

The maximum and the minimum value of temperature in post-monsoon months of October, November and December are 29.0°C and 17.0°C; 28.0°C and 8.0°C; 27.0°C and 5.4°C in the Sawai Madhopur district. During the same months, due to the start of winter, the temperature lowers down and the values of the mean monthly temperature recorded are 23.0°C, 18.0°C and 16.0°C, respectively.

FIG. 1.6

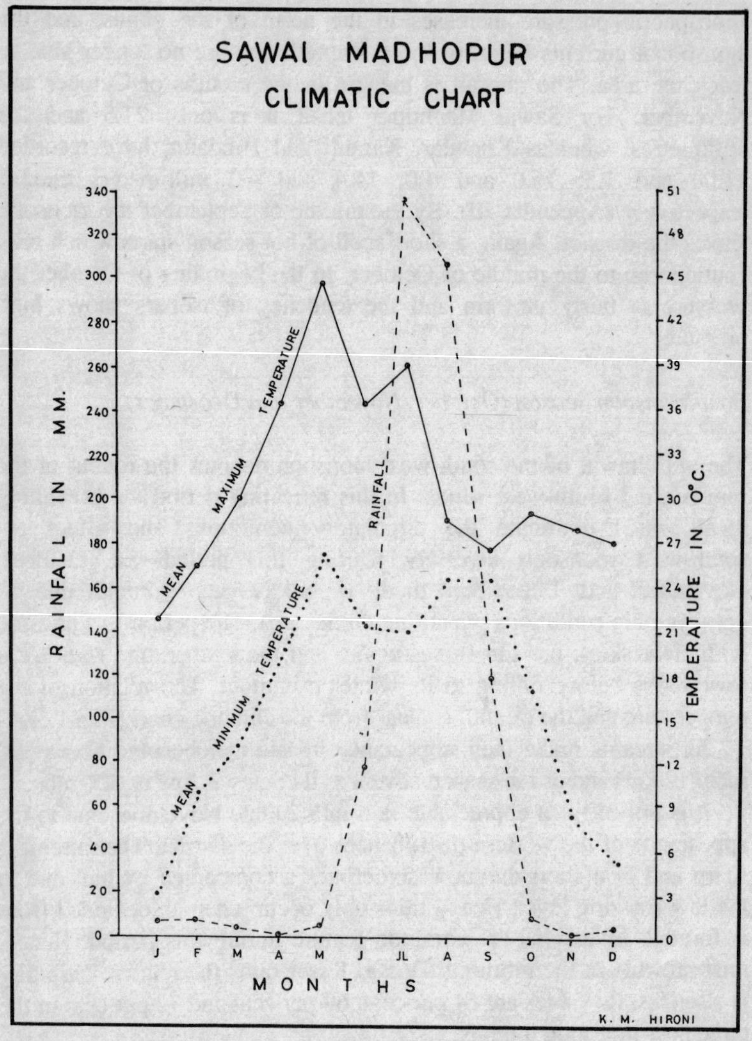

Winter (January and February)

January is a beautiful fine month in most of the region. By January and February the anti-cyclone establishes itself over Rajasthan and the temperate continental airmass which has now become cooler and drier prevails over the region. With the high pressure, the pressure gradient slackens and the temperatures are at their lowest, with January and February 22.0°C, 25.2°C and the lowest temperature recorded being 3.0°C and 9.0°C. During these two months the evaporation is 248 and 250 millimetres.

During this period the district receives scanty rainfall by the north-western disturbances. At Sawai Madhopur, Khandar, Todabhim and Karauli 8.0, 7.0, 11.0 and 11.0 millimetres rainfall was recorded in January, while 5.0, 3.0, 6.0 and 8.0 millimetres in February. But the maximum rainfall in 24 hours does not exceed 16 millimetres in the district.

The south, south-east and northern portions of the district are mostly hilly, and they are covered with dense vegetation. Due to thick vegetation on steep slopes and valleys, the concerned regions always remain covered with shade and further add to the coolness.

Due to the presence of water bodies and dense vegetation the relative humidity is also high and its values are 78.5 per cent and 72 per cent at Sawai Madhopur.

The Climographs (Fig. 1.7) of both the places – Kota and Tonk – indicate more relative humidity and more wet bulb temperature, i.e. muggy climate. Thus it can be concluded that the climate at both the places is not pleasant but habitable since a scorching type of climate is unbearable and more severe but a muggy.

Climate is less severe and therefore suitable for habitation.

Rainfall Intensity*

The rainfall intensity gives more accurate understanding than normal rainfall of an area, because of the fact that the amount of the rainfall received in a particular period proves to be more than the rest of the months. It is a device used to measure the concentration of precipitation at a particular place and in a specific period of time. The pre-monsoonal, monsoonal, post-monsoonal and winter rainfall intensities of 12 years of all tehsils have been calculated (Appendix IV). It has given a clear picture of the rainfall intensity and its subsequent effects on soil erosion and other hydrological parametres.

The value of mean dry seasonal intensity (Fig. 1.8) for Sawai Madhopur, Gangapur, Karauli, Boanli and Bamanwas being 3.13, 4.42, 3.4, 7.83 and 5.20 millimetres respectively. The monsoonal intensity

* Rainfall Intensity = $\frac{\text{Total rainfall}}{\text{Number of rainy days}}$

3.4, 7.83 and 5.20 millimetres respectively. The monsoonal intensity for the same tahsils accounts to 24.21, 24.55, 19.99, 22.5 and 24.42 millimetres, respectively which shows the concentration of rainfall is high in the monsoon season.

While considering seasonal intensity it has been observed that the winters intensity of rainfall is lesser in comparison to other seasons, its value being 4.81 millimetres, while in pre-monsoon it is recorded as 4.025, monsoon 20.87 and in post-monsoon season as a 4.904 millimetres.

FIG. 1.7

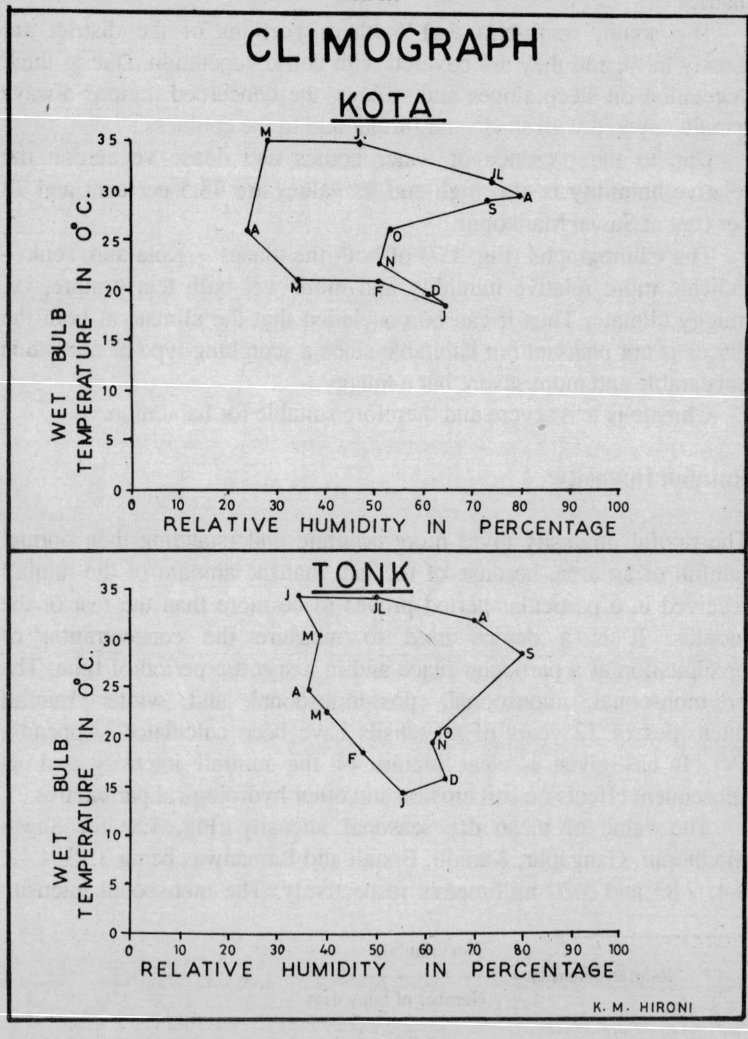

layers of these soils, the carbon contents, clay content and aggregation saturation capacity are comparatively lower than the lower layers. The above contention is verified from the fact that a zone of lime accumulation is found below one metre in the extreme south of the Sawai Madhopur district. In its north, down stream from the Banas water gap where moisture increases considerably, the depth of the calcium carbonate horizon in the alluvial soil of the valley also increases about two metres above. With the increase of moisture the aridity of the region tends to increase the mechanical weathering which is sometimes augmented by the short rainy season. This leads to shallow thickness of soil formation. A thin layer of *'kankar pan'* has developed in the soil. This again verifies the aforesaid fact.

Structure

The rocks of the area have been a source of material for soil formation. Main rock formations are of the Aravallis, the Gwalior and the Vindhyan system. When the soil is formed directly from the underlying rocks, the soil minerals present in the soil bear a direct relationship to the original rock. For example, the sandstones and limestones of the Vindhyan system are the meta-silicates of calcium, magnesium and iron. Most of these rocks, in this area, give rise to soils which are sandy in nature and comparatively poor in calcium content, generally reddish in colour. Over Gwalior, soils are greyish and clayey in texture. In Sawai Madhopur district the eastern and south-eastern portions have light black soils. Alluvial soil, in the area, is brought by rivers from the rocks of the surrounding areas, which are mostly of mixed mineralogy i.e. limestone, sandstone and shales of the Vindhyan system. The north western part is dominated by rocks of the Aravallis. Therefore, the rivers have brought soil from these sources.

Relief

Topography or relief of land is the condition which influences in more ways than the other factors of soil formation. The influence of topography, however, on the development of a soil profile, is observed in many of the localised depressions scattered all over the area. Water drained from the surrounding uplands collects in these lower depressions along with finer soil particles, making these soils in the depressions heavier in texture. The areas of Sawai Madhopur, Khandar and Karauli are mostly hilly having undulating topography. Therefore, the soils show varying degree of profile development. In the district the soils in the valleys, depressions at the foot of the hill slopes are deep, dark coloured and are heavier in texture. The soils on the hill slopes and upland are shallow, gravelly and light yellowish-brown to yellow. It is brown in colour.

Vegetation

In the district, the vegetative cover plays a significant role in reducing soil erosion, addition of the organic residues and development of the soil profiles. With the death of plants or shedding of leaves the process of humification and mineralisation gives rise to organic and inorganic acids and to the release of minerals present in the soils. Thus, plants act directly or indirectly as a factor of soil formation. Vegetative cover modify climate influence on the soils, especially, the erosion of the surface soil by water and wind is prevented. The plants and the layer of decaying organic matter, on the soil surface, trap the rainfall and reduce the direct effect of washing out of the soil with the flowing water. In the western and south-eastern parts of Sawai Madhopur, the vegetative cover plays a significant role in reducing soil erosion, addition of the organic residues and the development of the soil profile.

Time

Soil development goes through a time factor. But the duration of time cannot be measured strictly in terms of years, because, the time needed for a particular soil to develop depends on other factors of soil formation. For example, the soil development is more rapid in humid climate that supports good vegetation than in dry climate. Leaching plant nutrients are more rapid in a coarse-textured permeable parent material. Since this district is a part of multicyclic topography, hence polygenetic soils are evident in various parts especially on the plateau and hilly tracts.

SOIL CLASSIFICATION

The detail soil survey of Sawai Madhopur district has not been done so far, from the point of chemical and physical properties of soils. Only in some pockets, where irrigation projects have been introduced, the soils of such areas have been analysed, Marbut (1938), stressed upon the distribution between the dynamic (climatic and biologic) and passive (parent soil, topographic position and time) soil development factors. Again he revised the classification of the soils. He recognised the existence of three orders of soils: zonal, inter-zonal and azonal.

Zonal soils are formed through the prolonged action of climate and vegetation under the conditions of good soil drainage. Inter-zonal soils have followed the very poor drainage, on regolith with high calcium carbonate content, or where soluble salts, or sodium or both are high. Azonal soils have shallow thickness and do not possess a well developed profile because their existence is on the steep slopes.

Ganu and Moghe (1974) classified the soils of Rajasthan according to the American system of soil texonomy. It was followed on the basis of Thorp and Smith (1949) classification. It is based on a hierarchy of six categories or levels of classification: orders, sub-orders, great groups, sub-groups, families and series (Table 2.1). In the Sawai Madhopur district, out of five orders, only three groups and their sub-groups are present. The distribution and their characteristics have been discussed in the following pages with the approximate equivalents of old and new systems of soil classification.

TABLE 2.1: Soil Classification

Sl. No.	New comprehensive system		Great group	Approximate equivalent in the old system
	Order	Sub-order		
1.	Aridisols	Orthids	(a) Camborthids	Seirozems, desert soils
			(b) Calciorthids	
			(c) Salorthids	
			(d) Paleorthids	Saline soils of depressions
2.	Alfisols	Ustalfs	(a) Hapluslalfs	Red loam, black soils, brown soils, yellowish brown soils of foot hills, alluvial soils
3.	Entisols	Psamments	(a) Torripsamments	Desert soils
			(b) Quartzipsamments	
		Fluvents	(c) Torrifluvents	Alluvial soils
			(d) Ustifluvents	(old and recent)
4.	Inceptisols	Oehepts	(a) Ustochrepts	Brown soils, red and yellow soils of foot hills
5.	Vertisols	Usterts	(a) Chromusterts	Black soils
			(b) Pallusterls	

Shallow soils are present in the area approaching the hills. A large portion of the district is severely affected by water erosion problem. The land near the Chambal river has been converted into deep wide gullies. The area along the Banas and the Morel rivers is also suffering from this problem of erosion. Similarly, vast plain regions are also available in the district in addition to the eroded and shallow soils.

The representative profiles, from each categories mentioned above, are taken to describe each soil formation. The properties such as texture of surface soil, physiography of land, electrical conductivity, pH value and morphological characteristics of soils have been discussed.

Deep and Medium-black, Greyish, Dark-brown Soils

The heavier soils of the plain region of the district have been grouped together under this category. The soil of this class is deep and the colour generally varies from light-olive-brown to dark-olive and pale-olive-brown. The soils are of medium to heavy texture having moderate drainage. The soils are generally non-problematic, except in a few areas where the problem of salinity is present.

This class covers the tehsils of Nandauti and part of Bamanwas, Gangapur and Sawai Madhopur. The pH value of this zone generally ranges from 7.4 to 8.6 while the electrical conductivity varies from 0.3 to 5.5 m mhos/com. The description of a typical profile of the zone from Bamanwas village, is as given in the Table 2.2.

Deep Light-textured Yellow-brown Soils

A major portion of the plain region of the district is covered by this zone. The soil of the class is deep, light-textured i.e. sandy to loam and is yellowish-brown in colour. The soils are generally free from salinity-alkalinity problem except in a little area where this problem exists. This type of the soil is found along the flood plains of the Banas, the Morel and the Gambhir rivers and their tributaries.

The soils of this type are distributed in the major portion of the Mahuwa, Todabhim, Hindaun and Boanli tehsils. These soils are present, to some extent in Bamanwas, Gangapur and Sawai Madhopur tahsils of the district.

The description of a typical soil profile of this class is given in Table 2.3:

TABLE 2.2: Soil Profile Bamanwas (Bamanwas Tehsil)

Depth in cm	Morphological Characteristics
0-17	Brown (10YR 5/3 clay loam, blocky, structure, hard, thin and few roots. Moderately drained, no effervescence with dil HCl.
17-62	Dark greyish brown (2-5YR 4/3), clay loam, blocky, hard, moderately drained with mild reaction with dil HCl.
62-108	Dark greyish brown (2.5Y 4/3), clay loam, blocky and sun-angular, very hard, poorly drained, with moderate reaction with dil HCl.
108-above	Light olive-brown (2.5Y 5/4), clay loam to loam, massive structure, slightly hard, imperfectly drained, poorly effervescence with dil HCl.

TABLE 2.3: Soil Profile : Devali (Boanli Tahsil)

Depth in cm	Morphological characteristics
0-23	Strong-brown (7-5YR 5/6), loam, crumb friables, profuse roots, well drained, no effervescence with dil HCl.
23-63	Dark-brown (10YR 4/3), clay loam, blocky structure, hard moderate root distribution, drainage also moderate, no effervescence with dil HCl.
63-90	Yellowish-brown (10YR 5/4), sandy clay loam, sub-angular structure, friable, little few roots, moderately drained, no effervescence with dill HCl.
90-120	Brown (10YR 5/3), loam sub-angular, friable, few roots, drainage good, milk effervescence with dil HCl. Pinhead size Ca Co_3 nodules present.
120-162	Pale-brown (10YR 6/3), loam, sub-angular, friable, roots absent, poorly drained, tremendous effervescence with dil HCl. Peanut size Ca Co_3 concentration present. Salinity problem is under the developing stage at certain places of the tehsil.

Shallow-light Foot Hills Light-brown Soils

Shallow soils are scattered in almost all the tahsils of the district. A major portion of these soils are available near the foot hills of Karauli, Sapotra, Khandar and Sawai Madhopur tahsils. This soil is also present to some extent in the remaining of the tahsils of the district. Soils of this class are shallow to slightly deep. They are of light texture and yellowish-brown in colour. The depth of soils ranges from a few centimetres to almost bare rocks. The description of a typical soil profile is given in Table 2.4.

TABLE 2.4: Soil Profile : Karauli

Depth in cm	Morphological characteristics
0-20	Loam yellowish-brown, crumb structure, slightly Hard, profuse roots, drainage good, no effervescence with dil HCl.
20-45	Loam, yellowish-brown blocky less distinct structures, slightly hard, many roots, drainage good, no effervescence with dil HCl.
45 above	Sandstone rock, soil depth, is the main problem of the zone and as such most of the waste land area under this class is suitable for raising pastures.

Deep, Light, Ravined and Light-brown Soils

This class extends in Karauli, Sapotra, Khandar, Sawai Madhopur and Boanli tahsils of the district. The area adjoining the Chambal and the Banas rivers is eroded and gullied. This type of soil forms a considerable area of the district and has therefore, been placed in a separate group.

The soils of the area are very deep, non-calcareous, medium to heavy textured having moderate to severe erosion. On the basis of soil characteristics and land features the soils of this area have been classified into two subheads viz.:

- Moderately fine textured soils, and
- Medium textured soils.

Moderately Fine Textured Soils: These soils are deep to very deep, greyish-brown to dark-greyish-brown and moderately fine textured. They are located on gentle slope undulating lands and developed from alluvium. Those soils are well drained and calcareous. They are suitable for cultivating wheat, gram, barley, mustard, jowar, etc.

Medium Textured Soils: These soils are deep to very deep, well drained pale-brown to brown and medium textured. These are located on very gentle slopping (1-3%) to gently slope (3-5%) land and develop from recent alluvium. These soils are calcareous, pH value of the class is 7.70 and organic matter in the surface layer varies from 0.57 - 0.73 per cent. Description of a typical soil profile is given in the Table 2.5.

TABLE 2.5: Soil Profile : Pali (Khandar Tahsil)

Depth in cm	Morphological characteristics
0-20	Dark-brown in colour, loamy with crumb structure, slightly hard, many thin roots, well drained.
20-53	Dark-brown, loamy, composed structure (blocky and prismatic), slightly firm, a few thick and many thin roots, well drained, very few medium-white concretions.
53-96	Dark-brown, loamy, blocky, friable, few thick and thin roots, well-drained, very few medium white concretions.
96-137	Dark-brown, loamy, blocky, very few thick and thin roots, well drained, very few medium white concretions.
137-182	Dark-yellowish-brown, loamy tending to the massive, friable, very few thick and thin roots, well drained, many medium and few big white concretions, lime in powder form.

SOIL FERTILITY STATUS OF SAWAI MADHOPUR DISTRICT

Out of the eleven tahsils, soil samples received from ten tahsils were analysed for pH, EC, organic carbon content, available phosphorus and available potash by standard methods prescribed for soil testing in India, (1965 at the Soil Testing Laboratory, Durgapura, Jaipur). Soil samples were categorised into low, medium and high classes, as presented in Appendix VI. Fertility map (Fig. 2.2) of Sawai Madhopur district, on the basis of above data was prepared. Appendix VI shows the results of alkalinity, salinity problems and nutrient status of each tahsils is as follows:

Sawai Madhopur

About 25 per cent of the soil samples analysed in this tahsil shows the soils are high in phosphorus, very low in nitrogen and medium in potassium. Soils samples have salinity problem with only 1.4 per cent.

Boanli

On the basis of the 28 per cent of the total soil samples analysed, the tahsil is affected by salinity, since 16 per cent of the total soil samples show the above result. The soils are very low in available nitrogen but medium in available phosphorus and potassium.

Khandar

Fifteen per cent soil samples are affected by the sodic problem. There is no salinity problem but the tahsil is very low in nitrogen, medium in potassium and high in available phosphorus status.

Nandoti

The results illustrated that about nine per cent of the soil samples are affected by the problem of alkalinity and salinity. The tahsil is high in available phosphorus, medium in potassium and very low in nitrogen.

Karauli

This tahsil, too, is suffering from sodic problem and low availability of nitrogen, but it's medium in potassium and phosphorus contents.

FIG. 2.2

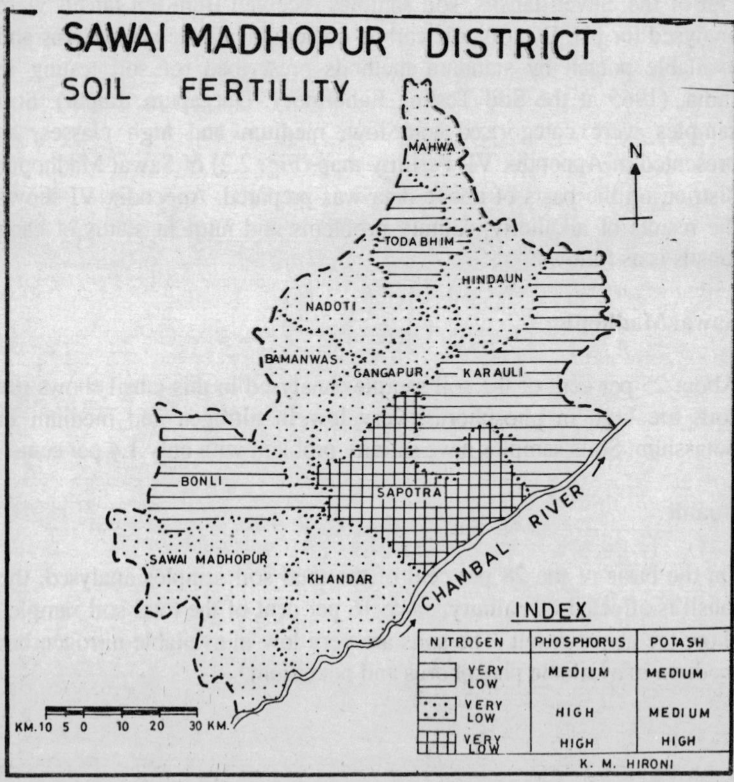

Todabhim

About 17 per cent and 75 per cent soil samples indicate the problem of alkalinity and salinity, respectively. The tahsil is low in nitrogen and medium in potassium and phosphorus.

Gangapur

The tahsil is deficient in available nitrogen, medium in potassium and high in phosphorus. It suffers with sodic and salinity problem with 20 per cent and 25 per cent soil samples, respectively.

Sapotra

The nutrient status of Sapotra shows very low in available nitrogen and high in potassium and phosphorous.

Hindaun

The problem of salinity is negligible while 22 per cent of the soil samples show sodic problem. The soils are very low in nitrogen, medium in potassium and high in phosphorous.

Mahuwa

Very low in available nitrogen while rich in phosphorous and potassium. Alkalinity and salinity problem are shown by 16 per cent and about three per cent soil samples, respectively.

3

FLUVIAL MORPHOLOGY

IN THE first chapter, it has been emphasised that geomorphic history of the study region is associated with the origin, upliftment, peneplain and rejuvenation of the Aravallis and evolution of the Vindhyan. The present topography is an outcome of a long but interrupted fluvial cycle of the Chambal, the Banganga and their tributaries. The post-Cretaceous history is linked with the orogenesis of the Himalayan mountain system. Various writers have pointed out that intermittent upheavals of the Himalayas have had profound influence on the evolution of the landforms of the marginal areas of the Peninsular shield. The region which is on the north-western margin of the peninsular shield cannot remain unaffected by such an epeirogenic effect. In the present chapter, therefore, an humble attempt has been made to discuss and analyse various aspects of fluvial features and to enumerate various evidences which may support the above contentions.

DRAINAGE BASINS

The drainage of Sawai Madhopur district can be classified into two drainage systems (Fig 3.1).

- The Chambal drainage system including the Banas and the Morel rivers, and
- The Gambhir system and its tributaries.

The Chambal Drainage System

The Chambal river forms the south-eastern boundary of the State of

FIG. 3.2

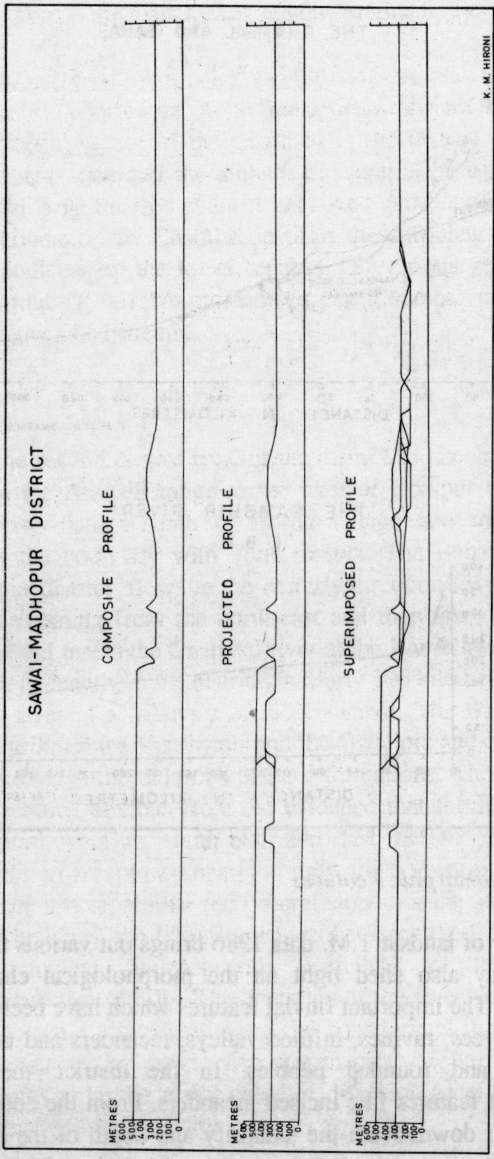
SAWAI-MADHOPUR DISTRICT
COMPOSITE PROFILE
PROJECTED PROFILE
SUPERIMPOSED PROFILE
METRES
600
500
400
300
200
100
0
FIG. 13
K. M. HIRONI

The structural and geomorphic evidences put forward by Sharma, indicate that the Banas river, during the Cretaceous period, diverted towards south as a consequence of which faulting provided weak zones and, consequently, favourable sites for river capture. In this way the waters of the Banas were captured by the Chambal system.

Heron (1938), Chatterjee and Bagchi (1957) are of the opinion that the Banas is an example of superimposed drainage. The Banas has cut across at four places throughout its course. In Sawai Madhopur the river has cut through the Vindhyan hills at Garh and Bhaopur in Khandar tehsil.

The course of the Banas throughout its long profile is meandering (Fig. 3.3A). It appears that once the river might have been flowing on the peneplain and the peneplain has been uplifted and the river has established its course on the same meandering course; as a result of upliftment, the course of Banas is incised. The Banas river is broad and braided near Bhagawatgarh and Haroti. Here the islands and rock outcrops at Padra and stony wastes near the confluence are observed. Besides this, the river shows other fluvial features like natural old levees, gullies, palaeo-flood plains and channel bars throughout the course.

The Gambhir River

The river originates at a place near the village Nindhar (altitude 411 metres) in Karauli tahsil of the district. It is an important right-bank tributary of the Yamuna. The Gambhir river carries most of the water of the extreme north-eastern part of the north-western termination of the Vindhyan basin. The river forms its present shape near the Panchna bridge. Here the river swallows the waters of five streams – Bhadrauti, Bhainsawat, Manchi, Barkheri and Atta. The river is named Panchai down-stream the Panchna bridge up to the Sonet railway bridge, and thence it becomes the Gambhir river. The Panchai is fed by small seasonal streams and not by any river of high magnitude up to the Katkar village. Namai is the only left bank tributary which runs parallel to the main river for 48 kilometres, originating from Chobe-ki-Gowan (altitude 355 metres) and joining the Panchai river near Merhi (altitude 234 metres).

The Gambhir stretches from its origin to Mundia loop, a channel distance of about 72 kilometres with an average slope of 2.61 metres in a kilometre. The Gambhir river takes an abrupt turn at this point and flows towards the east. This turn exhibits the change in the underlying strata and geomorphological features.

The river Gambhir flows on alluvium in most of its course except its right bank tributaries which flow mainly on the Vindhyan. This section of the river is characterised by the lateral and vertical erosion. An enormous quantity of load is carried over by the river. It has a capacity to transport cobbles, boulders, and even rock blocks of 1 to 2 metres diametre, down the Panchna bridge side.

The middle section of the river stretches within 77 kilometres from the Mundia loop to Nadi-ka-Gao loop. From Mundia (altitude 222 metres) to Nadi-ka-Gaon (altitude 183 metres) the average slope is 0.506 metres per kilometre. In this section the valley follows a more deformed zone and is traversed by the Great Boundary Fault. The Valley runs parallel to the Great Boundary Fault between the hills. After this region it leaves the district.

Long Profile of the Gambhir River

The long profile of the river (Fig. 3.3B) in its upper valley is concave but the major part of it is straight. This straightness of the curve and the lack of high waterfalls and structural discordance in the valley indicate the mature stage of the topography. Only in the recent past along the course of the rivers, the ravines and gullies have deepend due to incision. The valley does not experience well defined terraces or waterfall.

Valley Cross Profile

To elaborate the shape and morphometrical properties of the Gambhir river valley cross profiles were drawn. The data for the height of its banks were recorded at six places from Karauli down stream to Sri Mahaveerji and thus the average height was analysed. It shows asymmetrical shape of the Gambhir valley, since its left bank has 9.5 metres and right bank 12.7 metres height. The hard sandstone rocks formation scattered on the right bank can be one of the reasons for valley asymmetry. The small swift flowing channels from the Vindhyan escarpment have deposited alluvium and colluvium on the banks of the river.

Banganga in relation to structural trends of the area show a good correlation. The newly developing streams after the Mesozoic uplift adjusted to the underlying geological structure. But still, there are some pockets in the major rivers which do not show any accordance with the structure.

The structural control of the streams are of two types, firstly, the strike of the valley rocks, and secondly the tectonic disturbance in the region under study. The structural control of both the types can be seen in the area.

In the case of the Banas, it is mainly controlled by the strike of the country rocks as a subsequent stream. In the district the Vindhyan and the Gwalior formation run south-west to north-east along the Great Boundary Fault. In Sawai Madhopur the Banas river follows the outcrops of hard formation of the Vindhyan system.

The Banas first flows north-west to south-east direction and just before joining the Chambal it takes an abrupt turn nearly at a right angle towards the south. This direction is not after slope or strike of the rocks in the area. It seems, this diversion of the Banas indicates that once the Banas might have been flowing independently parallel to the Sawai Madhopur-Karauli line of hills. The diversion was followed either by tectonic movement along the boundary of the Vindhyans and the Gwaliors or by progressive streams piracy. The former seems to be the major cause of the change of its course.

Besides this, there are some sites in the major tributaries of the Chambal in the district where they do not follow the outcrops of the hard formation and they cut across the bold ranges through narrow gorge. These sites seem to be an example of super imposition.

From this view it can be inferred that the north-western tributaries of the Chambal as represented by the Banas may also have been formed as consequent streams on the north-eastern flank of the Aravallis and then came to be superimposed. It was due to the Aravalli it possibly arched up during the Mesozoic period.

The Gambhir river basin provides a unique example of the structural control over the flow and direction of streams. The Namai and Ghagar rivers follow the transverse fault. All the tributaries of this zone — Kakund, Nehro, Loheri and Kan, etc. — follow the main or parallel faults. Contrary to this the streams flowing from the Dangland and the Chambal scarp are obsequent in nature. Thus, it can be inferred that the tributaries of the Gambhir still have the same courses which they had at the time of the upliftment of the Vindhyans and the

Aravallis. The structural control due to tectonic disturbance is also evident in the rivers of the district.

DRAINAGE PATTERN

The adaptation of streams to the underlying structure makes the drainage pattern. The type of drainage pattern varies from place to place due to the influence of slope, lithology and structure. And finally, the study of the drainage pattern also helps in identifying the stage in the cycle of erosion.

The patterns of drainage in the Sawai Madhopur district are of four types:

– Dendritic pattern,
– Radial, centripetal patterns,
– Trellis pattern, and
– Rectangular pattern.

Dendritic Pattern

The only guiding factors for this pattern is the initial slope of the land. In the region of the Vindhyan formation between the north-western and the Bhandar escarpment, the general pattern of drainage is dendritic. The study of stream courses show that they are following the belts of structural weakness (joints and cracks).

This type of pattern may be noticed again in the western, south-western and eastern part of the district. South of Balwan Nadi, a tributary of Galwa (Banas), has formed a typical dendritic pattern (Fig. 3.4D), which indicates that the fluvial cycle of the Banas Basin has been encroaching to attain maturity.

Radial and Centripetal Patterns

This type of pattern covers a negligible area. But the domal structures initiate the pattern. In the south-eastern part of the district, due to the domal structure, there has been a tendency towards a radial pattern of drainage (Fig. 3.4A). The Gothra Bhumendra Sagar presents a typical picture of the centripetal pattern and just adjoining the hill Amarwar is a watershed between Karsil nadi and Bhumendra Sagar drainage which is again characterised by a radial pattern.

The areas of topographic high in the middle of the Ranthambhor plateau, with no strong local contrast in rock resistance formed of Upper Vindhyan sandstone shales and limestones of Vindhyan super group also exhibits the radial pattern in the district.

FIG. 3.4

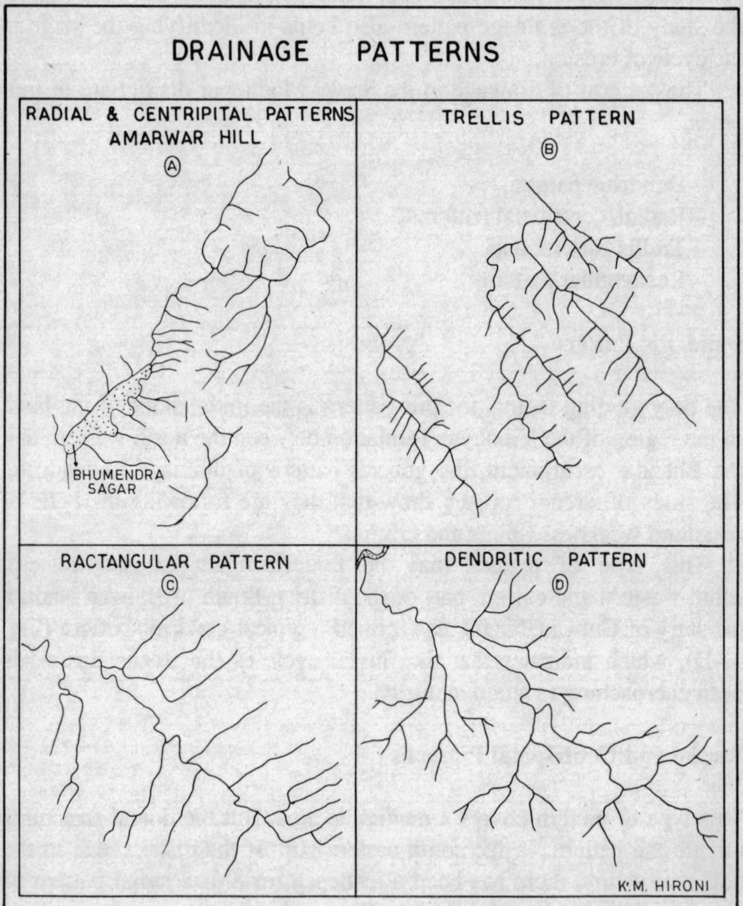

Trellis Pattern

In the Sawai Madhopur district the trellis pattern is very common in folded topography. This pattern shows sub-parallel stream, usually aligned along the strike of the Vindhyan rocks. Alternate bends of the Vindhyan sandstones and shales in this elongated belt provides a suitable condition for the development of the trellis pattern. It is fairly developed along the Sukh nadi, a tributary of the Karsil nadi (Fig. 3.4B).

Rectangular Drainage Pattern

In this case both the main stream and its tributaries display right angles bends. In the present case study of Sawai Madhopur the rectangular drainage pattern is noticed in the south-west of Chauth-ka-Barwara where the area is occupied with pre-Aravalli rocks (Fig. 3.4C). The rock structure of the south-eastern portion is well faulted and fractured; therefore, the stream courses are guided by them giving rise to the rectangular pattern. Machi nala, Tali nadi, Nahro nadi, Sesar nadi, etc. exhibit the rectangular pattern which may again be seen in the faulted area. Here the obsequent streams which descend from the scarp join the main stream at about right angle.

DRAINAGE FREQUENCY

Stream frequency is controlled by various factors, viz. climate, underlying rock and vegetation. Stream frequency is the number of streams per unit area which has been calculated for the present study by Strahler's method taking a unit of one square of two centimetres. The formula is as the following:

$$\text{Stream frequency} = \frac{\Sigma N}{A}$$

Where, ΣN = Total number of streams in the unit area, and
A = Area of the unit.

The streams frequency is governed by rainfall intensity, erosional proportionality factor, evaporation, infiltration rate, characteristics of rock and run-off.

It is clearly portrayed by the map (Fig. 3.5) that a high degree of streams frequency lies in the south and south-eastern parts of the Sawai Madhopur district. Here the Banas river takes a turn towards the south, near Haroti. From this place downstream the frequency increases tremendously. Looking at the geological formation in this part of high frequency it is observed that the area is covered by the lower Rewa sandstone and Kaimur sandstone mostly of Upper Vindhyan Group on the left bank, while on the right bank the shales and quartzite of Gwalior system and the Bhandar sandstone are the chief formations. Another area of high streams frequency is obvious near Bhagwatgarh and Chauth-ka-Barwara to the south of the Banas river. This area is composed of pre-Aravalli hills. The stream frequency in the district ranges between a minimum of zero to a maximum of 1.4 per unit. The total range of stream frequency in the district has been divided into three categories — low, medium and high which are given in Table 3.1:

TABLE 3.1: Stream Frequency Distribution

Sl. No.	Size class	Frequency	Cumulative frequency	Frequency (%)	Category	Cumulative (%)
1	0-0.25	189	189	44.15	Low	44.15
2	0.25-0.50	150	339	35.04		79.19
3	0.50-0.75	66	405	15.42	Medium	94.61
4	0.75-1.00	19	424	4.43	Medium	99.04
5	1.00 and above	4	428	0.93	High	100.00

Table 3.1 illustrates that most of the frequencies are concentrated in the low category. The detail description is given in following paragraphs.

The Areas of Low Frequency

The areas below 0.5 stream frequency, lies in the northern, eastern, southern and the south-eastern portions of the district. The category of low frequency covers a significant area of about 79.19 per cent of the total area. It shows the fact that this category covers the maximum area of the district and mostly occurs on the plain and foot hills areas of the district, which are composed of alluvial soils.

The Areas of Medium Frequency

The category of medium frequency consists the third and the fourth class sizes and falling on about 19.85 per cent of the total area. Two areas can be identified in this category. First, in Karauli a considerable area along Panchai and Manchi nadi and, second, along the Banas river on both the banks and the hilly areas of Sawai Madhopur and Khandar tahsils. Here the correlation between high stream frequency, high drainage density and ruggedness is very much clear. The whole area is broken with ravine and gullies.

FIG. 3.5

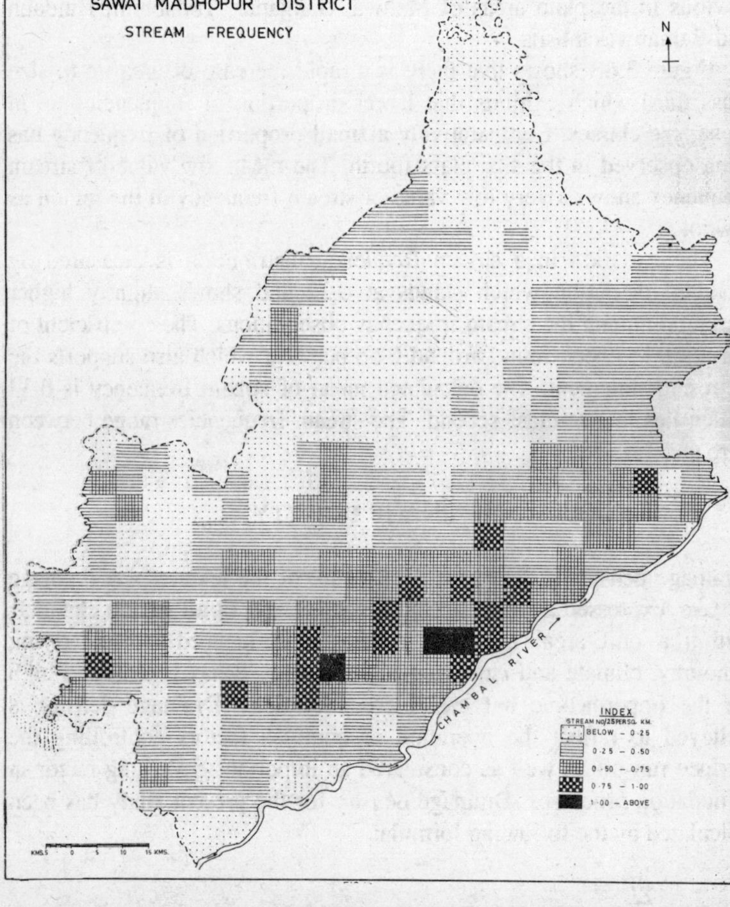

Areas of High Frequency

The last category covers an area of merely 0.93 per cent with the stream frequency of 1.00 and above. This category falls almost in the areas of high altitude e.g. near Ranthambhor and Bhagawatgarh. Another area of this category lies near the confluence of the Banas with the Chambal. The area is covered with limestones of the Vindhyan system, which is more prone to erosion hazards.

Figure 3.6A reveals that the distribution of steam frequency is quite uneven. The lower categories share a major part of the region which is obvious in the plain areas of Mahwa, Gangapur, Todabhim, Hindaun and Bamanwas tahsils.

Figure 3.6B shows that there is a rapid increase of area up to size class third which exhibits that larger proportion of frequencies lie in these size-classes. Comparatively a small proportion of frequency has been observed in the size class fourth. The mean low value of stream frequency shows a very low value of stream frequency in the region as a whole.

The variation in a stream frequency distribution is measured by standard deviation which stands at 0.22 and shows slightly higher variation among the stream frequency observations. The co-efficient of variation has been found around 0.66 per cent which also supports the aforesaid statement. The calculated mean of stream frequency is 0.33 which lies in size-class second. The stream frequencies range between zero and 1.4.

DRAINAGE DENSITY

Drainage density is defined as a measure of the texture of a drainage system, expressed as the ratio of the total length of all stream channels within a unit area. Drainage density is influenced by underlying lithology, climate and character of the terrain. It has been found high on the impermeable but easily erodible rocks. Drainage density is believed to reflect the operation of complex factors controlling the surface run-off as well as considered an important governing factor in denudation processes. Drainage density for the present study has been calculated by the following formula:

$$Dd = \frac{\Sigma L}{A}$$

FIG. 3.6

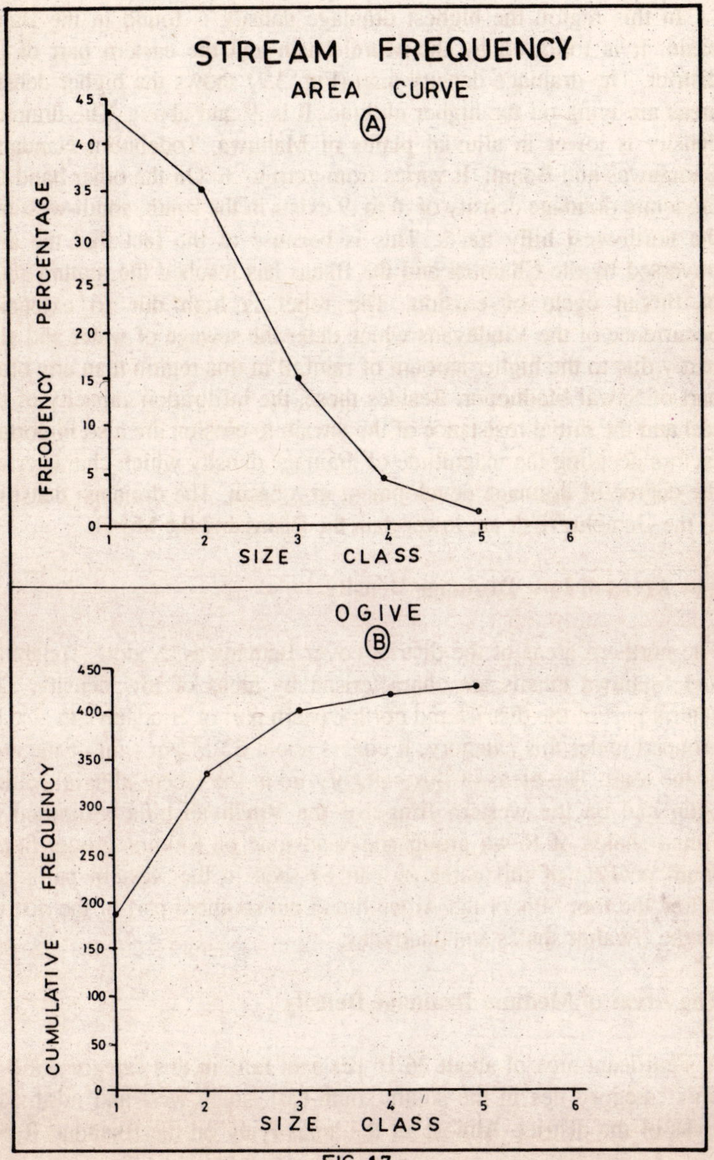

STREAM FREQUENCY
AREA CURVE
A
FREQUENCY PERCENTAGE
45
40
35
30
25
20
15
10
5
0
1
2
3
4
5
6
SIZE CLASS
OGIVE
B
CUMULATIVE FREQUENCY
450
400
350
300
250
200
150
100
50
0
SIZE CLASS

FIG. 17

Where, Dd = Drainage density,
ΣL = Total length of stream channels in a unit area, and
A = Area of the unit.

In this region the highest drainage density is found in the Banas basin. It is followed by the Morel basin and the eastern part of the district. The drainage density map (Fig. 3.7) shows the higher density areas are lying on the higher altitude. It is .9 and above. The drainage density is lower in alluvial plains of Mahuwa, Todabhim, Nandauti, Bamanwas and Boanli. It varies from zero to .6. On the other hand the moderate drainage density of .6 to .9 exists in the south, south-west and the north-west hilly tracts. This is because of the fact that the area traversed by the Chambal and the Banas has reached the mature stage of fluvial cycle of erosion. The relief is high due to extensive occurrence of the Vindhyans which deter the sewage of water and also partly due to the higher amount of rainfall in this region than any other part of Sawai Madhopur. Besides these, the infiltration capacity of the soil and the initial resistance of the terrain to erosion are also important factors deciding the magnitude of drainage density which characterises the degree of drainage development in a basin. The drainage densities of the Gambhir river are lower than the Banas and the Morel.

The Areas of Low Drainage Density

The northern areas of the district cover Bamanwas, Nadoti, Todabhim and Mahuwa tahsils are characterised by areas of low density. The central part of the district and north-eastern part of Hindaun can also be grouped under this category. It covers about 62.14 per cent of the area of the total. The areas of this category lie in the recent alluvial rolling plain and on the western fringe of the Vindhyan hills composed of Panna shales of Rewa group and sandstone of Kaimur group. Some small pockets of this category can be seen in the western parts just below the foot hills of the Aravalli and the southern part of the district on the Gwalior shales and quartzites.

The Areas of Medium Drainage Density

A significant area of about 26.16 per cent falls in this category of 0.9. This category lies in the south, south-east, south-west and north-east areas of the district. Almost all the areas lying on the Bhandar, Rewa and Kaimur groups of the Vindhyan System are mainly composed of sandstone, shale, panna, and conglomerate rocks. But in the south-west this size class rests upon the rocks of gniess and schist of the Aravallis. A small pocket of this category can also be seen on the Alwar series in the western part of the district.

FIG. 3.7

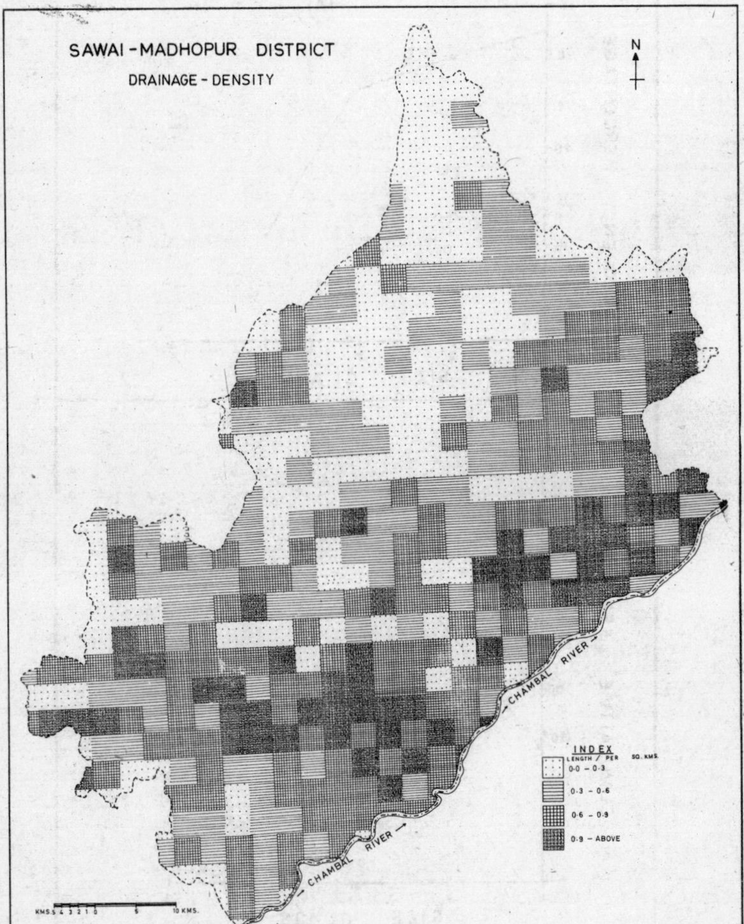

FIG. 18

FIG. 3.8

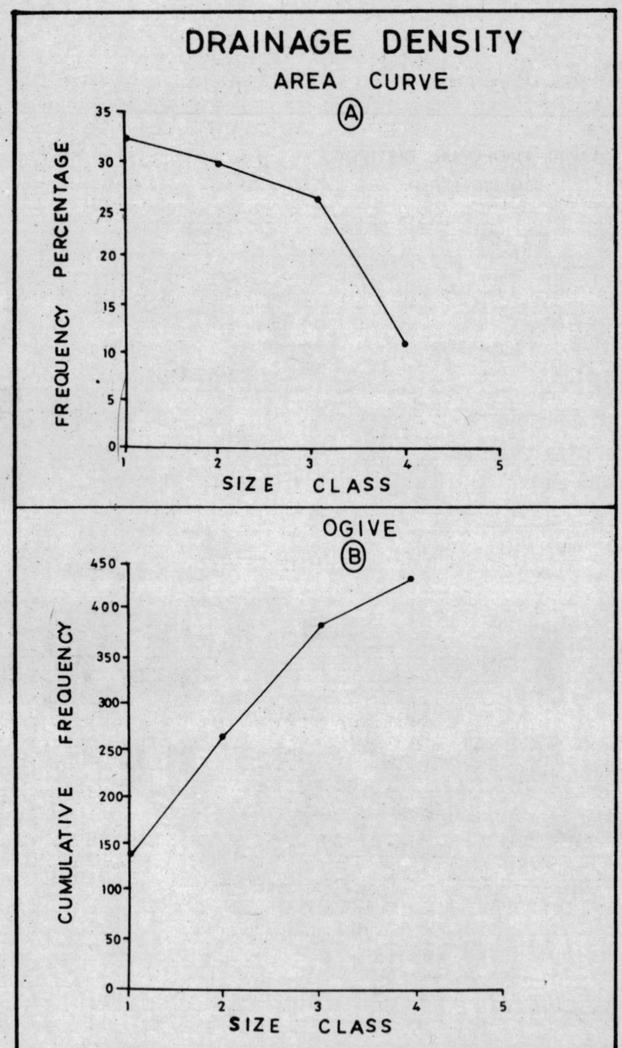
DRAINAGE DENSITY
AREA CURVE
A
FREQUENCY PERCENTAGE
35
30
25
20
15
10
5
0
1
2
3
4
5
SIZE CLASS
OGIVE
B
CUMULATIVE FREQUENCY
450
400
350
300
250
200
150
100
50
0
1
2
3
4
5
SIZE CLASS

FIG.19

TABLE 3.2: Frequency Distribution of Drainage Density

Sl. No.	Size Class	Category	Frequency	Cumulative frequency	Frequency (%)	Cumulative (%)
1	0-0.3	Low	138	138	32.24	32.24
2	0.3-0.6	Low	128	266	29.90	62.14
3	0.6-0.9	Medium	112	378	26.16	88.3
4	0.9- above	High	50	428	11.68	100.00

The Areas of the High Drainage Density

This size-class covers an area of 11.68 per cent covering an area of 1,250 sq km. It has comparatively, a different position. In the south this category generally lies in the Banas Valley while in the north it lies between Dang areas where the Bhandar limestone is common. In the south the category is resting upon alluvial plains.

The area and drainage density curve Fig. 3.8A shows a negatively skewed distribution of drainage density. The drainage density portrays that there is a gradual decrease from first size-class to fourth size-class. The concentration of frequencies in the first to three size-classes, are high.

The variation among the drainage density values as measured by standard deviation shows the value of .30, indicating high variation among observations. The calculated coefficient of variation at .6 per cent confirms the validity of this result.

4

FLOOD MORPHOLOGY

RUNNING WATER is responsible for sculpturing the landscape more than any other surface process. Rivers erode their valleys and, in the process, provide a system of drainage that is delicately balanced with the climate, topography, rocks and soil. Defining a flood is difficult, partly because, floods are a complex phenomenon and partly because they are viewed differently by different people. The term 'flood' frequently connotes that a stream or a river has reached a high water condition likely to cause damage to personal property on the flood plain. The definition given by Rostvedt *et al.* (1968) is that "A flood is any high stream flow which develops natural or artificial banks of a stream". Various researches have given divergent views on the incidence of floods. Enendu (1981) based his analysis on the monthly rainfall records and basin slope characteristics, Rodha (1969) is of the opinion that short term rainfall characteristics such as storm size, intensity and duration and channel slope rather than basin slope prove more significant which explain the incidence of floods. Source areas may develop in other parts of the catchment than the valley bottoms and lower slopes. Thus, Hewlett and Nutter (1969) suggested that the source area expansion would reach quickly into areas with shallow soils and bare rock surfaces, while some are of the opinion that hollows and slope profile concavities, in addition to the base of slopes and areas of thin or less permeable soils, would rapidly become saturated during storm precipitation.

FLOOD INCIDENTS IN SAWAI MADHOPUR

Documentary sources on Sawai Madhopur floods are few. Many historians from the erstwhile States of Karauli and Jaipur have opined that these states have been prone to floods; statistics of 1804 and 1812 prove this. James Todd, in his book *Annals of Antiquities of Rajasthan* has produced revealing facts about the floods in Sawai Madhopur district. Even in the recent past the district witnessed five floods in twelve years.

Between 10 July and 12 July 1968 heavy rain fall was recorded to the tune of 310 mm within 48 hours. As many as 221 villages and 11,252 people were affected by the floods. Many parts of the district and the Sawai Madhopur town were innudated. A loss of 2,060 livestock was recorded. 720 houses collapsed involving a loss of Rs. 8.30 lacs.

In 1969 the district witnessed another fury of the floods. The primary cause of this flood was heavy rainfall on 13 and 14 August 1969 in the tahsils of Nadoti, Karauli, Hindaun and Gangapur. In Karauli 8 inches of rainfall was recorded in one day resulting the Gambhir river to overflow. Statistics show 146 villages, 1,800 houses, 3,444 families and 22 livestock affected by the flood.

Again, in 1971 the tahsils of Khandar, Sawai Madhopur, Boanli, Gangapur, Hindaun, Karauli and Sapotra were severely affected by floods. The chief cause was heavy rainfall amounting to four times the average in the months of June and July. The rainfall was recorded at 36 mm in Sawai Madhopur, 25 mm in Khandar and 31 mm at Gangapur in 24 hours. It brought the Morel and the Banas rivers in Spate. At Karauli and Sapotra 319 mm rainfall was recorded in 6 days in the month of June and 458 mm of rainfall in 13 days in July. This caused Panchna and Gambhir rivers to rise rapidly.

The year 1972 saw yet another flood fury in Sawai Madhopur district on 11 and 12 August. Hindaun, Gangapur, Nadoti and Karauli received 315 mm, 483 mm, 604 mm and 571 mm of rainfall, respectively. As a result many dams were breached in the tahsils of Gangapur, Bamanwas. Nadoti, Hindaun, Todabhim, Mahuwa, Karauli and Sapotra. This fiood affected 534 villages and 18,538 acres of agriculture land.

Flood of 1981

The year 1981 saw unprecedented floods in the district. This was caused by heavy rainfall that lashed the districts of Tonk and Jaipur between 17 and 20 July 1981. The Morel dam was washed away causing the Banganga, Bhadrawati and Borkheda rivers to overflow.

Besides this, due to unabated heavy rainfall all lakes in the tahsils of Bamanwas, Hindaun, Gangapur, Karauli and Boanli were overflowed and breached. On 19 July, the Morel dam was washed away at three places, flooding 36 villages of Boanli; 10 villages of Bamanwas and another 10 villages of Sapotra (names of affected villages are given in Appendix VII and their locations in Fig. 4.1).

The lake in Siwad village of Sawai Madhopur, Nagar and Nangal dams of Tonk district were washed away causing floods in the Galwa rivers. This affected 10 villages in the Boanli tahsil extensively. The villagers of Piplia and Mahapura were evacuated.

In Khandar tahsil the Banas river was flooded causing a nullah to change its course which accelerated the surge of flood.

In Todabhim tahsil 20 villages were washed away and 12 lakes overflowed as a result of heavy rainfall. Eight villages were affected when the canal from Jagram was breached. Mundia village was filled with sediment deposits by the flooded Gambhir river.

Floods occurred severely on 19 July in Hindaun town and another 12 villages of the tahsil. Jat-ka-Talab and Jalshen were opened due to heavy continuous pressure of the water.

In Mahuwa tahsil the Nagrampura canal lent an increased force to the flood in the river Banganga. About 400 families in the tahsil were severely affected by floods in 10 villages.

In Sapotra tahsil four villages were affected due to floods in the Morel and the Karsil rivers. About 53 lakes were overflowed.

Unceasing rainfall endangered four villages in Gangapur tahsil. The flood was as a result of breaches in Khandeep and Telenwala lakes. During the floods on 18, 19 and 20 July, 172 mm, 166 mm and 163 mm, rainfall, respectively, was recorded. Thirteen villages in Bamanwas tahsil were affected in 1981.

In this flood the Morel dam was breached which washed away Berkhandi village besides causing extensive damage in many villages. On 17, 18, 19 and 20 July, 270 mm, 255 mm, 505 mm and 208 mm, rainfall, respectively, was recorded. This caused breaches in 65 lakes of Lalsot tahsil; 640 families and 11,256 people were affected. The loss of livestock was put at 647.

In Nadoti tahsil six villages were affected by the flood. This flood was caused due to breaches in Nadoti, Tesgoan and Handaheli lakes.

Appendix VII shows the flood affected villages (tahsil-wise) and Table 4.1 reveals the damages and loss by 1981 floods.

Damages and Loss by 1981 Floods

Loss to Agriculture: Much damage was done to crops and livestock due to wide spread and heavy rainfall. Crops ready for harvest in 59 thousands hectares land were destroyed. Another 0.04 hectares agriculture land was rendered unfit for cultivation due to sediment deposits carried by flood water.

FIG. 4.1

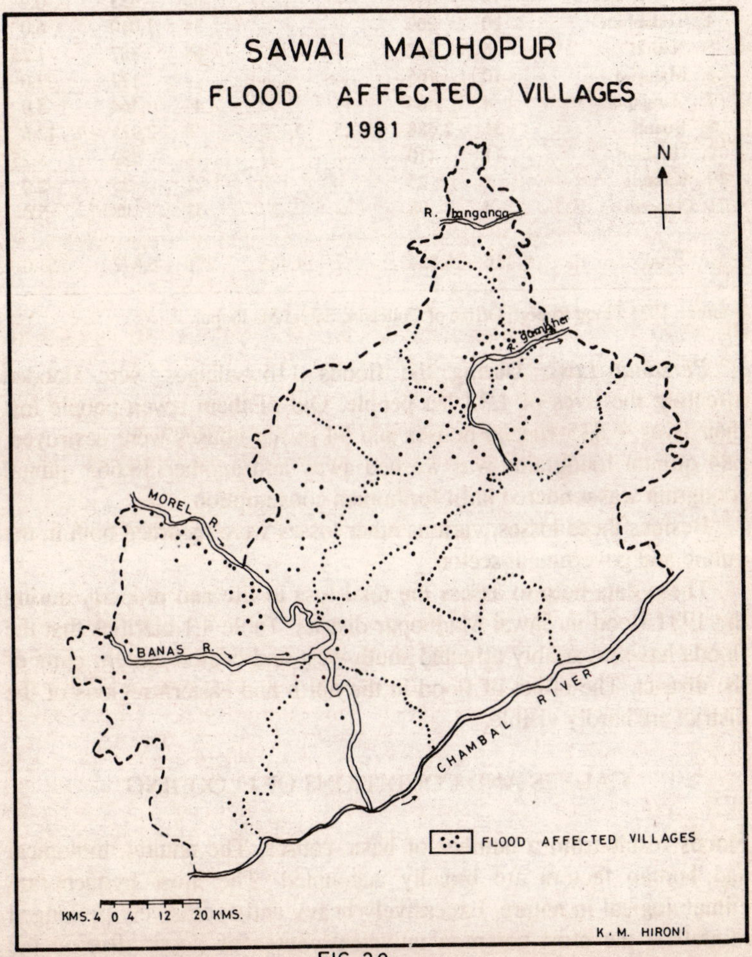

FIG. 20

TABLE 4.1: Damages and Loss by 1981 Flood

Name of tahsil	Number of Villages affected	Number of families affected	Human loss	Live-stock loss	Number of dams/tanks affected	Number of houses affected	Crop loss area '000 ha
1. Sawai Madhopur	10	773	2	464	—	555	5.0
2. Khandar	1	15	—	—	—	15	3.0
3. Bamanwas	13	640	—	647	68	633	0.9
4. Todabhim	20	969	—	—	34	1,010	6.0
5. Nadoti	6	307	—	82	68	387	1.25
6. Mahuwa	10	165	—	—	—	172	7.0
7. Gangapur	4	464	—	35	44	464	5.0
8. Boanli	36	2,688	5	3,125	4	2,921	12.6
9. Hindaun	11	410	—	47	8	532	5.25
10. Karauli	1	25	—	3	22	25	2.0
11. Sapotra	4	98	—	27	53	98	5.0
Total	116	6,554	7	4,425	271	6,672	53.0

Source: 1981 Flood Report, Office of Collector, Sawai Madhopur.

Personal Loss: During the floods 116 villages were flooded affecting the lives of 1.33 lac people. Out of them seven people lost their lives, 6,635 *kuccha* houses and 94 *pucca* houses were destroyed, 684 quintal foodgrains was washed away and another 38.663 quintal foodgrain was rendered unfit for human consumption.

Besides these losses, various other losses were recorded both in the public and government sector.

These data help to assess the total loss to life and property during the 1981 flood in Sawai Madhopur district. Table 4.1 clarifies that the floods have invariably affected south-west and central eastern parts of the district. The effect of flood in the north and eastern regions of the district are hardly visible.

CAUSES AND CONDITIONS OF FLOODING

Floods result from a number of basic causes. The natural, biological and human factors are broadly accounted. The most frequent are climatological in nature. Excessively heavy and excessively prolonged rainfall is the most common universal causes of floods. But on the other hand heavy rainfall is not the only factor which is responsible for floods. Sometimes it is observed that one place get higher rainfall but there is no flood and the other places which receives lower rainfall may create flood. Besides the heavy downpour topography, slope, geology, drainage system, runoff and discharge, drainage density, soil and vegetation are equally responsible for flooding. In addition to these aspects, the landuse and human interferences in the catchment area also have its own responsibility in flooding.

Climatic Factors

The network and channel slope conditions, do not cause floods; they are rather flood accelerating conditions. Ultimately, the location of the district falls in semi-arid tract where floods will be rainfall induced. Therefore, the rainfall of different sizes was analysed for mean intensity, seasonal intensity and the duration of the rain. These factors prove more significant in explaining the proportion of rainfall that goes into run-off (over flow and through flow).

The statistic of year-wise rainfall intensity (Appendix V) shows that all the tahsils of the district have four months of rainy season with a high frequency of heavy rainfall in which no flood occurred regularly. But all the tahsils of the district had copious and wide-spread rainfall in 1972 and 1981 and vast areas were affected by it. And these two years were the flood affected years. Thus, the antecedent weather conditions and storm condition during floods are pertinent in order to understand as to how the heavy rainfall is predisposed towards flooding within the district.

If looking at the daily statistics of the rainfall recorded in the district in 1981 (Table 4.2) one finds that in Bamanwas tahsil 270 mm rainfall was recorded in one day (on 17 July). This was 20 per cent of the total rainfall recorded during the month. On 19 July it was 505 mm which constituted 40 per cent of the rainfall during the month. Other tahsils witnessed heavy rains. Too much of rainfall in an equally small period of time caused the river to innundate and the dams to breach in 1981. Mahuwa tahsil was the only exception where there was less than average rainfall. It remained unaffected by floods. To comprehend further the character of Sawai Madhopur Floods, the storm conditions during floods, were analysed (Fig 4.2).

Table 4.2 shows that more rainfall was received in a short span in 1981. The monsoon months of June, July and August faced more than normal rainfall. In Bamanwas the rainfall was 1,444 mm, more than the average while in Karauli tahsil it was only 29.5 mm in excess. Also, all these areas that witnessed heavy rains in July are situated in the west of the district.

TABLE 4.2: Rainfall (in mm) Account from 1 June 1981 to 15 August 1981

Tahsil	Average rainfall	From 1-6-81 to 6-7-81	Daily rainfall from 17-7-81 to 21-7-81					Total rain-fall from 1-6-81 to 15-8-81
			17	18	19	20	21	
Sawai Madhopur	768	115	6	26	43	62	29	526
Khandar	664	137	3	24	22	52	18	452
Boanli	725	261	28	154	264	131	31	1,127
Gangapur	958	237	—	127	166	163	11	1,036
Bamanwas	399	—	270	255	505	208	13	1,543
Nadoti	477	150	8	72	175	173	1	867
Hindaun	556	82	5	30	130	300	12	1,029
Mahwa	508	99	—	—	166	—	—	669
Todabhim	688	192	—	49	71	308	12	896
Karauli	705	182	13	84	84	120	2	739
Sapotra	846	126	—	56	56	135	166	966

Source: 1981 Flood Report, Collector Office, Sawai Madhopur.

As a measure of the antecedents weather conditions, the water-budget graph of Sawai Madhopur was plotted, based on the methods of Thornthwaite (1948). The major criticism against the Thornthwaite method is that its potential evapotranspiration (PE) estimated is based on a temperature dependent formula and therefore the PE estimates are lower in the dry season but higher during the rainy season (Garnier, 1968 and Olaniran, 1981). Nevertheless, the approach retains validity in depicting the seasonal trend in soil moisture status. Thus, the water surplus depicted by the graph (Fig 4.3) will first be utilised in recharging the underground moisture reserve from May and should be available for rapid run-off from about August to October.

Temperature

Temperature controls the amount and the rate of evaporation in flood prone areas. Evaporation may often have far more decisive effects on outflow then the rainfall does in the district during April, May and June, the average temperature rises up to 44.5°C. As a result, high evaporation takes place and the soils of the area bear high rate of infiltration. But during the rainy season (July-September) these temperatures range from 26°C to 29°C and lower down the rate of evaporation which ultimately contribute to the intensity of flood.

Discharge and Run-off

It is established fact that the load carried by a stream is controlled largely by turbulence, which in turn, is associated with discharge. It is

FIG. 4.2

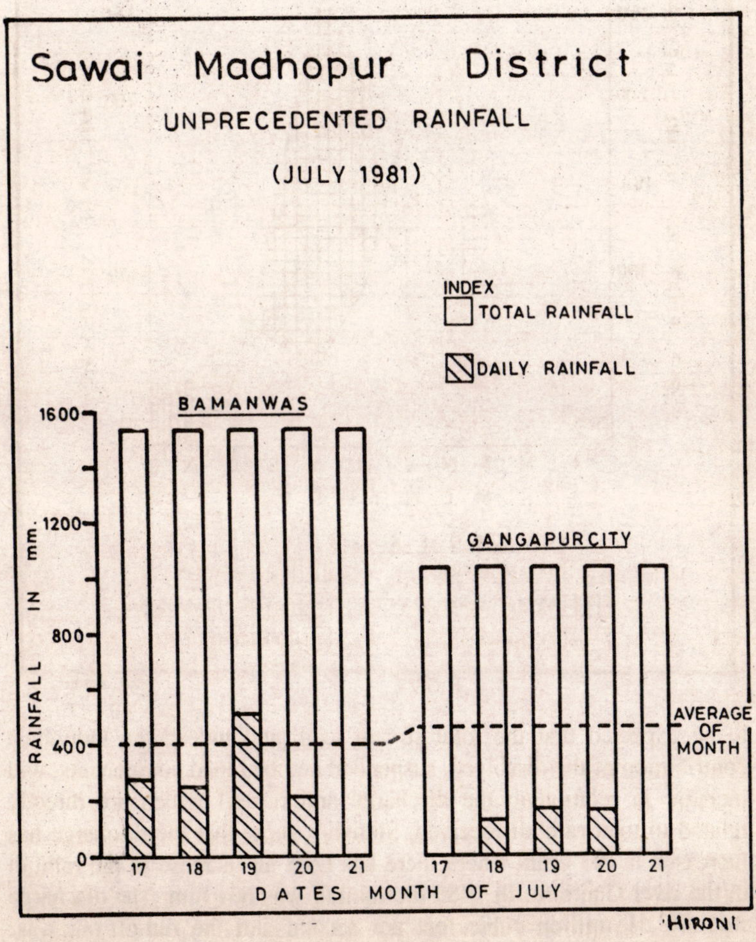

FIG. 4.3

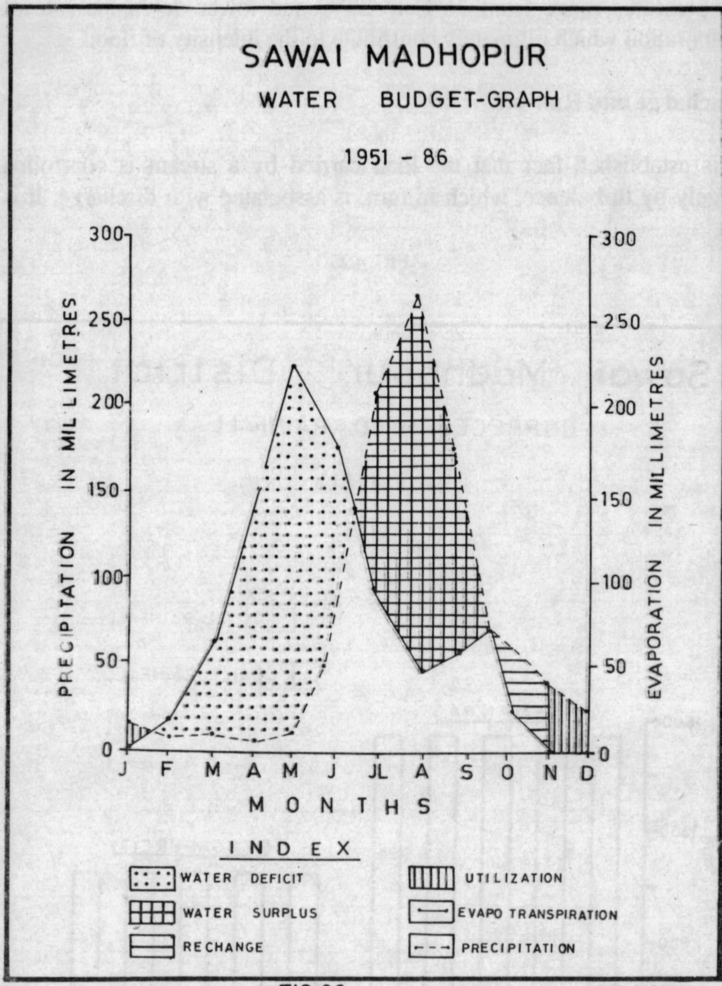

FIG. 22

to be expected that the total stream load, and indeed the individual contribution of the dissolved, suspended and bed load components, will increase in relation to the discharge and run-off which are directly related to total rainfall received. Statistics show that the discharge has increased in the years where there has been an increase in the rainfall in the river Gambhir. In 1980 the rainfall was 601 mm. The discharge was 143.51 million cubic feet per second and the run-off rate was

FIG. 4.4

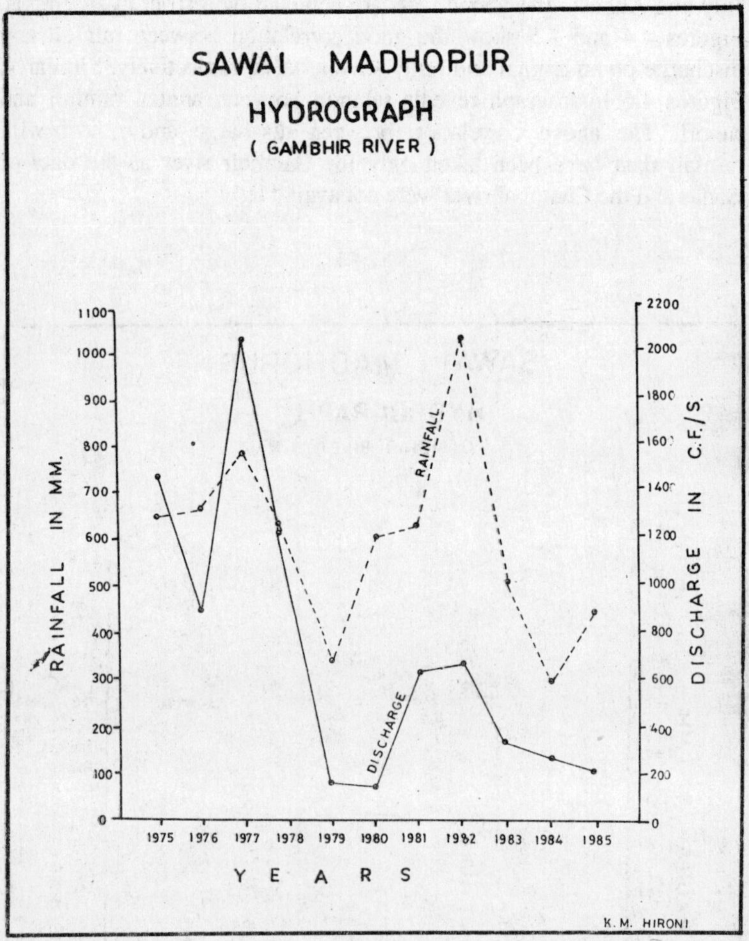

155.49 million cubic feet per second. In 1981 the rainfall increased to 626 mm, thereby, increasing the discharge to 630.40 million cubic per second. This shows that the discharge rate was affected not due to the rainfall in the district, but also in the adjoining areas. This shows the intake capacity of the river, causing floods. Taking the data into account, one finds that the average rate of discharge and runoff during the monsoon is 135.78 and 49.00 million cubic feet per second, respectively. The same is enhanced to 257.00 and 127.00 million cubic feet/sec in July and 409.13 to 203.00 million cubic feet/sec in August. After August it tends to recede. This factors contributes to the floods in July and August. The above facts are depicted by district hydrographs. Figures 4.4 and 4.5 show the good correlation between rainfall and discharge on an annual and rainy season basis, respectively. Similarly, Figures 4.6 hydrograph reveals relation between annual rainfall and runoff. The above correlation between discharge and runoff with rainfall data have been taken only for Gambhir river as the data of Banas and the Chambal river were not available.

FIG. 4.5

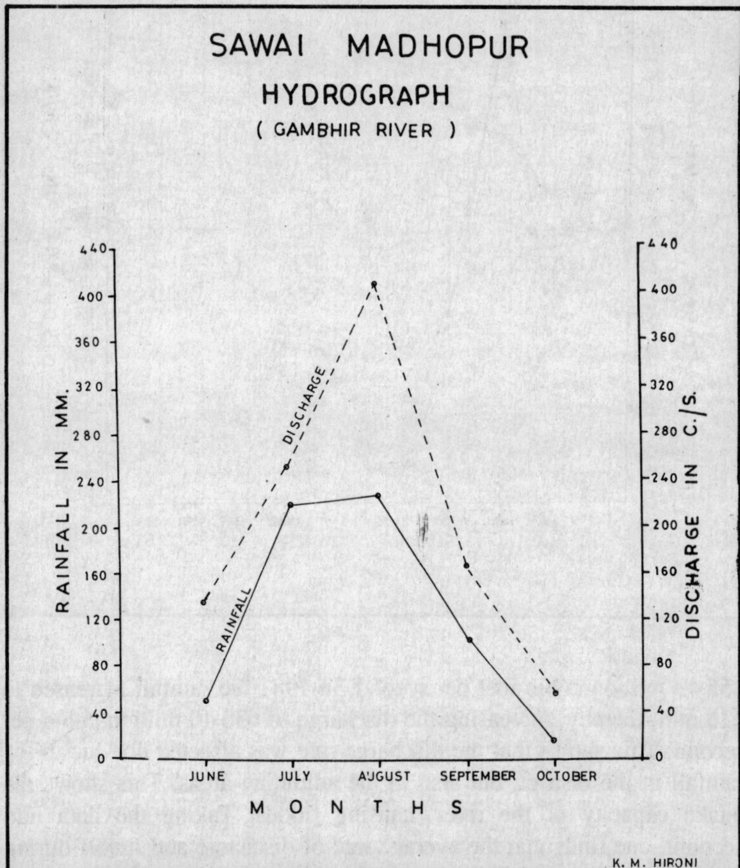

Heavy rainfall is not only factor which is responsible for flood. The drainage system and topography of an area are equally important factors. Flood does not mean heavy rainfall.

Topography

In Sawai Madhopur the floods are witnessed in the alluvial plains between Aravalli hills in the west (300 metres) and Vindhyan hills in the east from 450 to 600 metres. The alluvial plain has 200 to 220 metres average height from mean sea level. The general slope is west to east and in the north-east the slope is south to north-east.

Therefore, the low lands of alluvial are highly prone to floods. The Banas, the Morel and their tributaries bring their turbulent waters and accumulate it in the low lands of Boanli, Bamanwas, Gangapur, Nadoti, and Sawai Madhopur tahsils. Thus the basin which is more or less in circular shape is highly vulnerable to flooding. Here several tributaries like Galwa and Gambhiri streams join the Banas while Kareli and Karsil streams join the Morel. These streams collectively cause high-magnitude flood peaks. With the prolonged rainfall conditions, the number of major tributaries have a greater flood potential near Haroti.

In the north and north-east the Gambhir river and its tributaries like Manchi, Panchai, and Atta etc. taking water from the Dangland creates flood in Todabhim and Hindaun tahsils with less intensity in comparison to the Banas and the Morel rivers.

Banganga brings water from higher altitude (360 metres) of Rajgarh, enters in Mahuwa Plain (altitude 200 metres) and causes floods comparatively even in low rainfall due to slope gradient towards the tahsil.

In the hilly region – Sawai Madhopur, Karauli and Sapotra tahsils remain free from flood threats because of the slopes that carry away the water to distant levels at a fast pace. It is evident from the floods of 1971 and 1981, that the tahsil of lowland areas between the structural hills were the highly affected ones.

Geological Factors Affecting Discharge

Rock structure and lithology greatly influenced the water discharge at any particular segment of a river. In the area of permeable rocks the surface runoff is low as the infiltration capacity of the terrain is high. The eastern portion of the district does not witness widespread floods, firstly, because from the confluence of the Banas, towards the north-east to Dholpur, the areas are scattered and occupied with limestones of Bhandar group, which absorb the water through infiltration. Thus it curtails the flood water, secondly, in the west of the Chambal river, the area is being fringed by the steep rock walls of the Vindhyan sandstones. Therefore, numerous swift flowing *nullahs* and stream pour their water directly into the Chambal river and do not pose threat of flood. Thirdly, the presence of numerous clefts and joints in the sandstone of the eastern fringe of the Vindhyan. The infiltration rate is high and the amount of surface run-off is low and as a result the tributaries of the area do not show high discharge.

The impermeable Jhiri and Panna shales of the western slopes of the Vindhyan hills and hematite shales of Alwar series in the east, provide a high percentage of surface run-off to the alluvial plain lying between and at times make serious floods in this central portion of the district.

Palaeo-Drainage and Flood

The abandoned channels are always vulnerable to floods. These areas are of high soil moisture and hold immense potential for groundwater. During flood palaeo-channels reactivate themselves and accelerate the flood situation.

In the present study area, there are numerous evidences of the migration of the Banas and the Morel rivers. Sharma, H.S. (1984) has clearly deciphered the palaeo-channels of the Banns and the Morel and other rivers on landsat imageries and aerial photographs supported with field evidences like fluvial sand mixed with gravel, natural old levees, gullies, palaeo-flood plain. Further he advocated that disorganised and abandoned channels of these streams which get reactivated and create flood hazards during the rainy season. Figure 4.8 depicts palaeo-channels of the Bannas which has migrated southward (Sharma, 1984). It has been pointed out in the previous chapter that the Banas was formerly an independent river flowing across the Karauli plateau toward the north-east. But as a consequence of the great boundary fault movement the river got diverted towards the south taking an abrupt right angle turn and joined the Chambal. The abandoned drainage along the sharp turn of the Banas and the existence of the palaeo flood plain on the Karauli plateau further support the thesis.

FIG. 4.6

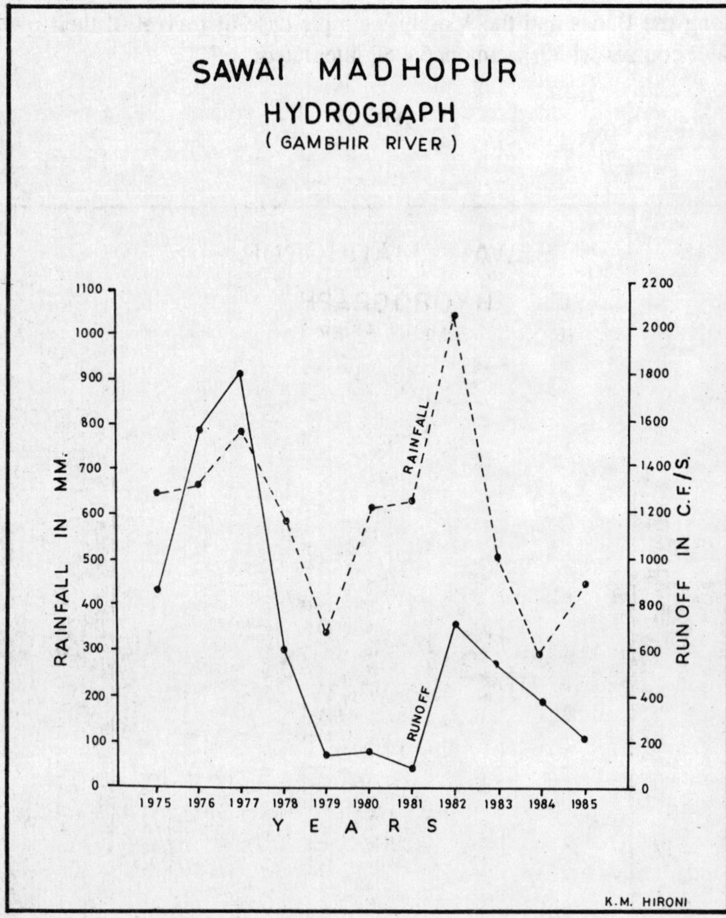

The entire area between the Banas and the Morel and the south of the Banas always faced worst flood hazards. Since here the courses, which were totally disorganised before floods, on which extensive farming was being practised, got revived during the floods perhaps due to heavy demand on the main channel. The study of landsat imageries and field evidences bring out the fact that the Gambhir was once the major right bank tributary of the river Banganga (arrow river) which in turn is now a major right bank tributary of the Yamuna.

It will thus be clear from the above evidences that the flooding along the Banas and the Morel, is simple case of revival of their own older courses which were once well integrated.

FIG. 4.7

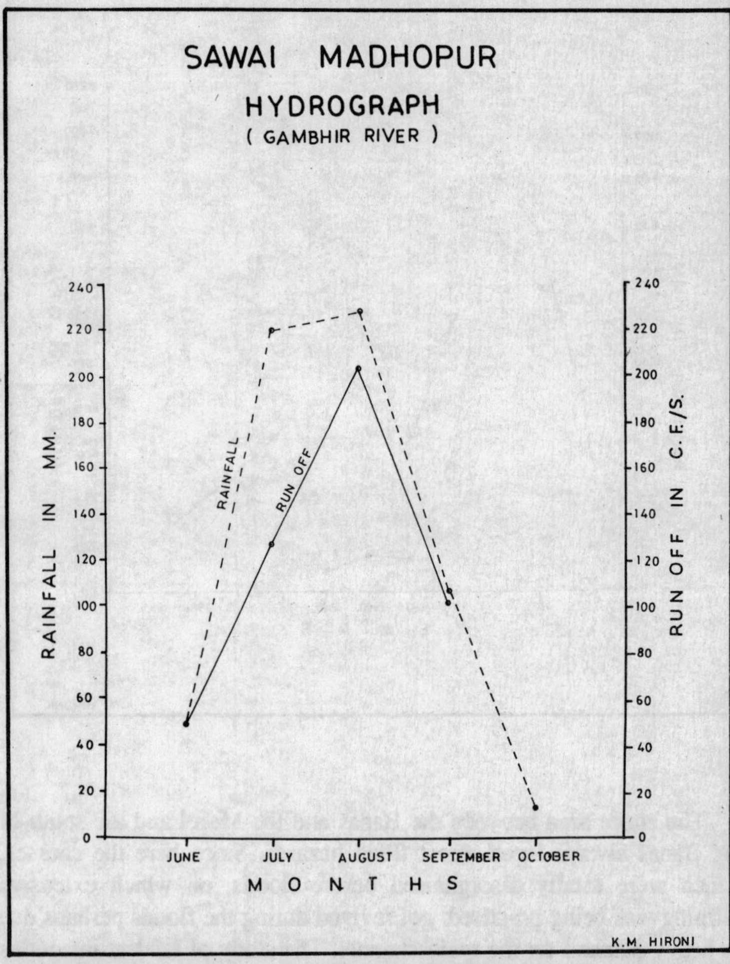

FIG. 4.8

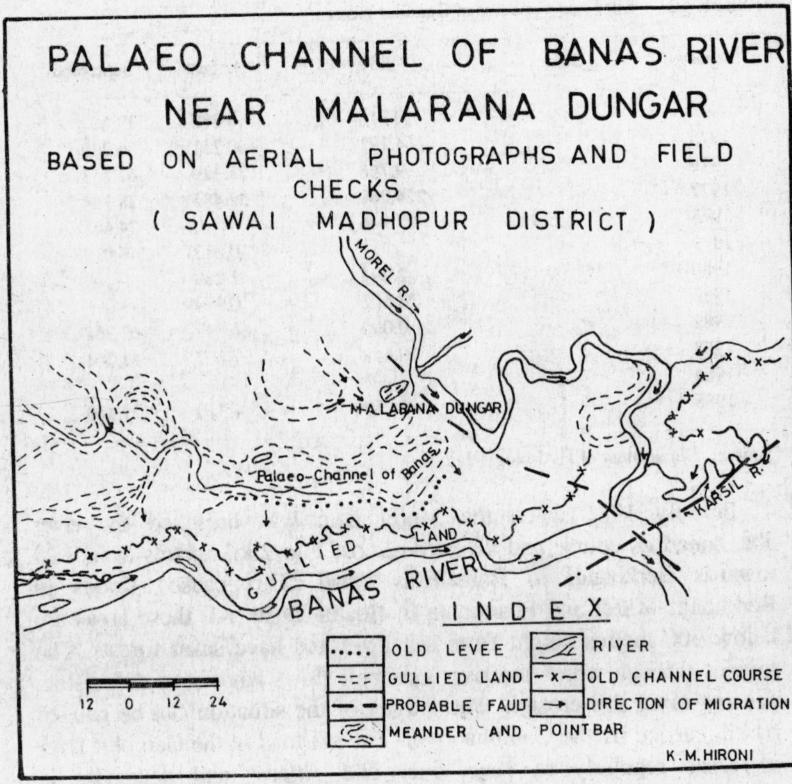

Vegetation

The vegetation cover on one hand increases the rate of infiltration of soil and on the other it checks the erosion hazard and high flow of water. Sawai Madhopur district has 22.5 per cent under forest of the total geographical areas. The dense forests are found in Sapotra (52%), Karauli (40.6%), Khandar (34.79%) and Sawai Madhopur (19.69%) tahsils. Therefore, these areas are free from flood hazards.

Continuous destruction of forests within past 20 years has resulted in the soil erosion along the river banks accelerating condition of flooding.

TABLE 4.3: Silt Load Capacity of Gambhir River

Year	June	July	August	September
1974	—	10.718	8.883	19.60
1975	—	164.191	100.251	6.239
1976	—	9.748	127.729	62.853
1977	—	224.050	52.485	28.134
1978	13.980	87.146	—	24.663
1979	—	—	0.0137	0.0137
1980	0.797	2.294	2.289	—
1981	—	27.602	0.9799	—
1982	—	0.090	66.737	67.368
1983	—	10.442	7.807	13.561
1984	—	—	—	—
1985	—	2.059	4.710	7.439

Source: Department of Hydrology, Jaipur.

In July 1981 when the Morel dam was breached the river abandoned its course and diverted almost 1 to 2 kilometres to its east towards Berkhandi in Bamanwas tahsil. This caused floods in Berkhandi, Karel and Phalmanta in Boanli tahsil. All these areas are below 300 metres height from sea level and have scant forests. The ravines through which the river Gambhir flows have been deforested, causing rapid soil erosion. The gravity of the situation can be gauged by silt carried by the Gambhir river. The silt load in the Gambhir river increases regularly in June, July and August and decreases in September (Table 4.3).

5

RAVINE MORPHOLOGY

VAST LITERATURE is available dealing with the problem of ravine and gully erosion in the arid and semi-arid regions of the world. In India, very scant attention has been paid on the morphological study of ravines and gullies.

Among the many types of soil erosion the earth scientists are largely concerned with the relatively important geological erosion and accelerated erosion. The land being eroded without the interference of human activities is considered as geological erosion. When man alters the ecosystem by various landuse practices, it increases the rate of erosion and this is called accelerated erosion. Ravine cut landscapes occur in many areas and have many names. The French call them lavaka, the Brazilians vossoroca or boccoroca (Tricart, 1972; Pradini, 1974; Okafiori and Soares, 1976). They have been reported from Zimbabwe (Stocking, 1978), Madagaskar (Petit and Borgeat, 1965), Central Russia (Bogolyubova and Karaushev, 1979) and many parts of the American south-west where they are associated with the name 'arroyo' (Cooke and Reeves, 1976) and (Martin J. Haigh, 1984). In a country like India where the pressure on land is very high, she can ill afford the luxury of leaving these areas as wasteland. Ravines are spread over an estimated area of 3.67 millions hectares along the rivers and their tributaries in India. The National Remote Sensing Agency, has estimated nearly four million hectares of land under ravine land in the country on the basis of landsat data. More serious ravine erosion problem occurs along the banks of the Beas (Punjab), the Chambal (Madhya Pradesh, Rajasthan and Uttar Pradesh), the Kalisind, the Banas, the Morel and the Gambhir (Rajasthan), the Yamuna (Uttar Pradesh), the Mahi, the Sabarmati, the Narmada and the Tapti (Gujarat) and their tributaries.

FIG. 5.1

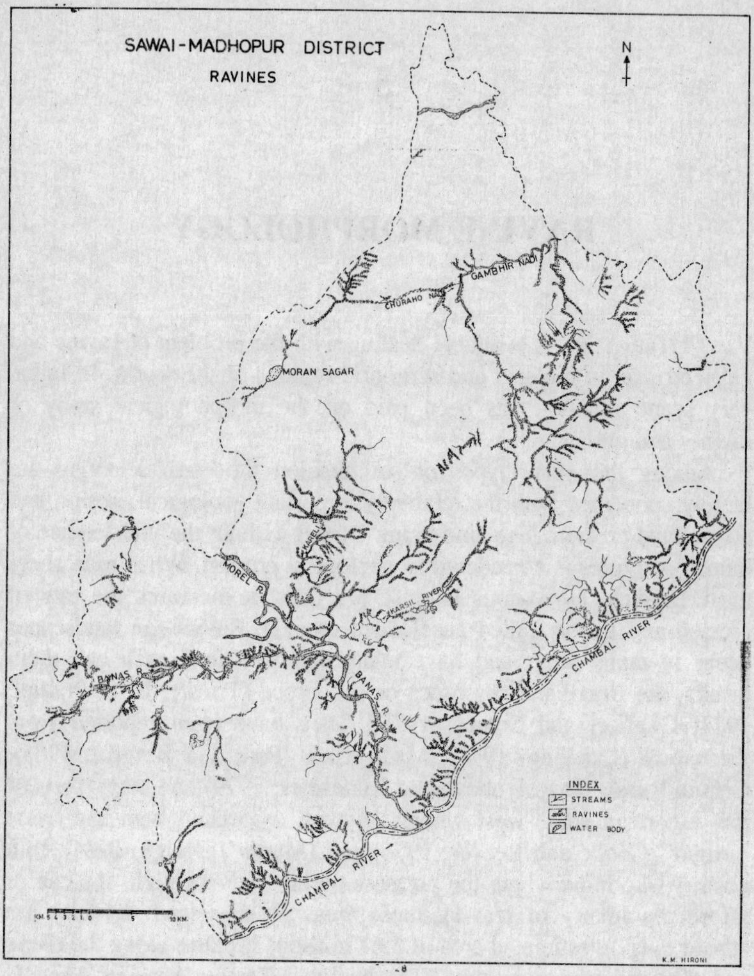

Vast stretches of land along the banks of the rivers of Sawai Madhopur district, namely, the Chambal, the Banas, the Morel and the Gambhir and their tributaries are affected by severe gully erosion (Fig. 5.1). There is even now a large land of the district where sheet erosion is going on year after year, unnoticed, till gully formation starts and large areas of valuable cultivated lands are converted into gullies and wasteland. So many villages on these river banks had been shifted in the past and are shifting even now due to this menace.

Except a few isolated works, no serious effort has been made to study these lands. The study of the ravines has been taken up by Bryan (1925), Horton (1945), Leopold Wolman and Miller (1966), Graf (1979), Denevon (1967), Cooke and Reeves (1976), in American and European countries. In India Tejwani, Dhurva Narayan (1960), Yadav (1961), Ahmad (1968, 1970), Sharma (1968, 1970, 1976 and 1980), Verma (1969), Seth *et al.* (1970) and Bali (1972) have tried to find out the causes of ravine formation.

Sharma (1980) in his pioneer work *Ravine erosion in India* has defined 'ravine' as, "A channel of ephemeral flow, denuded and guided essentially by the process of rejuvenate streams, and having steep sides and head scarp with a width and a depth always greater than a gully." He further clarified the morphological character of a ravine and a gully. Generally, a gully initiates along the animal trails, roads and paths on the agricultural uplands. On the other hand, a ravine begins along the river sides and encroaches upon the catchment area by headward growth.

DISTRIBUTION OF RAVINE AREAS

The study of ravine affected areas is a significant aspect of fluvial geomorphology. On the basis of the intensity of ravine erosion rates and morphological characteristics, the areas of ravines erosion in the district can conveniently be divided into four major zones:

- The Gambhir-Panchai-Manchi Ravined Area
  (Zones of severe ravine erosion),
- The Banas-Chambal Confluence Ravine Area
  (Moderately severe ravine erosion),
- The Morel-Banas Ravined Area
  (Moderate ravine erosion), and
- Scattered Ravine Areas
  (Insignificant ravine erosion).

The Gambhir-Panchai-Manchi Ravined Area

The ravine areas extend from 240 to 260 metres from mean sea level along the Gambhir river, while Panchai and Manchi ravined areas stretch from 260 to 300 metres. The area falls over Vindhyan sandstone, shale and quartzite. Most of the ravines are concentrated between the hills of Dangland (Fig. 5.2). The ravines along the Gambhir river are evident at Sri Mahaveerji, Merhi, Randoli on the left bank and Sanet, Katkar, Bari Rond on the right bank. The depth of the ravines is normally 15 to 20 metres. But it exceeds even to 20 metres along the Bandhwa Nala. The bedland topography is more pronounced along the Panchai Nadi and the Manchi Nala. In the Karauli tahsil between two Dangs the whole areas has been converted into a bedland by small *nullahs* and tributaries. The Chandur *nullah* between Teli-ki-Panseri and Liloti Dang, the Manchi *nullah* between Manchi and Atta Dang and the Atta nadi and Dhoblavala between Atta and Lador main dang, are notorious in their erosion capacity. The depth of the ravines vary from 15 to 25 metres in this area. Sometimes the length of a ravine reaches up to 3 to 5 kilometres.

The Banas-Chambal Confluence Ravined Area

It is a moderate to severe ravine affected area. The area stretches over the southern part of the Dangland. The whole area between the foot of the Chambal scarp and the Chambal river is engulfed by ravines (Fig. 5.3). The Banas joins the Chambal river downward towards Barwas near the Rameshwar Ghat. The zone is stretched on a height of 200 to 220 metres from mean sea level and the depth of the ravines varies from 15 to 20 metres. The length hardly exceeds 5 kilometres.

The ravine erosion is also evident along the right bank of the Banas at Gokalpur, Singor Kalan and Akoda villages. Between the Chambal and the Banas rivers the area is highly dissected.

The south of the confluence of Narar Khal, Narala and Pali are accountable for ravine topography along the left bank of the Chambal river. The depth of ravines here varies from 5 to 10 metres. But it increases towards the Chambal river.

The Morel-Banas Ravined Area

The ravine cut in recent and sub-recent alluvium is common in this area. Here two compact ravine zones are obvious:

- The area between the Bassi-Jatwara and Boanli hills is at an elevation from 300-360 metres, along the Morel and its tributaries.
- The lower Morel river is below 180-190 metres.

The Ravine of the Morel between Bassi-Jatwara and Boanli Hills

The ravine erosion is quite active by the streams that descent from the Boanli hills. The upper reaches of Morel are moderately affected. Here the depth is generally 10-15 metres. The head scarp is vertical while the side scarp is comparatively gentle.

The Ravines of the Lower Morel and Its Tributaries

The tributaries of the Morel that descent from the Vindhyan scarp form bedland features along the lower reaches of the Morel. Due to different layers of soils the side scarps are not regularly steep, but head scarps are usually steep. The depth is more than 20 metres.

FIG. 5.2

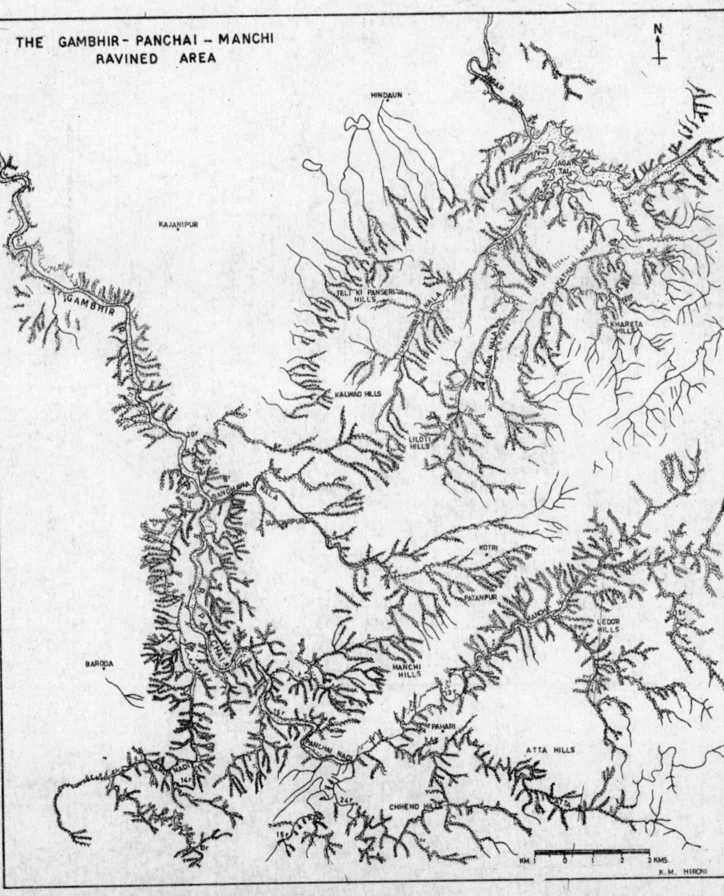

FIG. 5.3

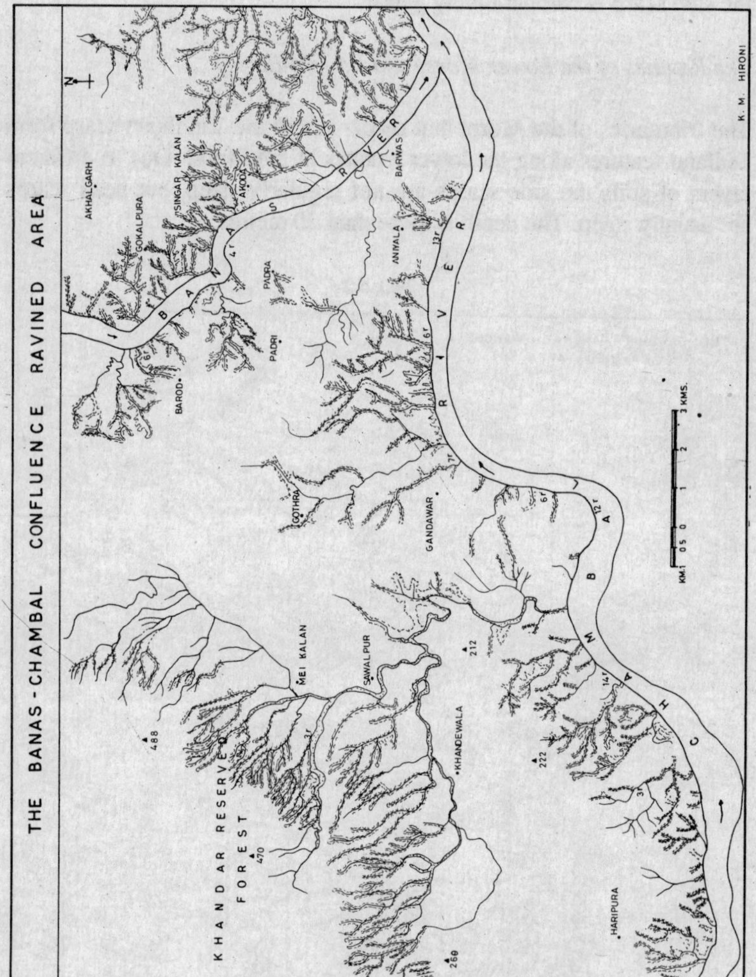
THE BANAS-CHAMBAL CONFLUENCE RAVINED AREA
BANAS RIVER
CHAMBAL RIVER
AKHALGARH
GOKALPURA
SINGAR KALAN
AKODA
BARWAS
ANIWALA
PADRA
PADRI
BAROD
GOTHRA
GANDAWAR
MEI KALAN
SAWALPUR
KHANDEWALA
KHANDAR RESERVED FOREST
HARIPURA
488
470
212
222
KM. 1 0.5 0 1 2 3 KMS.
K. M. HIRONI

The Banas and its tributaries are also attended with bedland erosion. The small stream which descends from Bhagwatgarh, having an elevation of 400 metres is characterised with ravines of 10-15 metres depth.

The Scattered Ravine Areas (Insignificant Ravine Erosion)

Relatively small patches of ravine areas are also found at many scattered areas specially along the Bhain-ka-Nala and the Kareli nadi which are the tributaries of the Morel. The streams descending from Dabra and Garain hills are also in the process of ravine erosion north of the Sapotra town.

CLASSIFICATION OF RAVINES

A systematic method of ravine classification is necessary for evolving suitable methods of ravine erosion control and reclamation. Hence, ravine and gully erosion is the function of soil type, geology, character of streams, rainfall, slope and upliftment. The study of ravines in the middle Chambal Valley, the Banas, the Morel Basin and the Gambhir basins in Sawai Madhopur district indicates that the said character and thickness are the major governing factors of morphology, size and areas pattern of the ravines. In this area gullies have been classified on the basis of their form, gully head characteristics (e.g. in plan and longitudinal section), length, breadth, depth and catchment.

According to their respective shape the ravines may be classified (in order of their developmental stage) as: (i) linear, (ii) bulbous, (iii) compound, and (iv) trellis. The long and narrow ravines (linear in form) usually formed along the natural drainage lines after progressive transformation under aggravated soil erosion conditions bifurcate into branches and develop "bulbous" shape. These bulbous ravines after enlarging into compound ravines in turn join the main drainage channels as tributaries at right angles. This shape is termed as "trellis" shaped ravines.

Numerous attempts have been made to group gullies into classes and prescribe treatments accordingly, but too many variables need to be considered. The treatment of a gully depends on gully location and dimensions; side and longitudinal channel slope; size; shape and prevailing slope, cover and drainage conditions of watershed: and ultimate use to be made considering scientific and economic feasibility.

In India, different types of gully classification are being followed in the ravine infested states in northern India. Tejwani (1961), has classified lands into four classes and has taken into consideration depth, bed width and side slopes of gullies which are given in Table 5.1.

TABLE 5.1: Gully Classification (Tejwani, 1961)

Symbol	Description		Specifications		
			Depth	Bed width	Side slope
G_1	Very small gullies		3 m	18 m	Varying
G_2	Small gullies		3 m	18 m	Varying
G_3	Medium gullies		3-9 m	18 m	8-15 %
G_4	Deep and narrow gullies	a.	3.9 m	18 m	Varying
		b.	9 m	Varying	Varying
			(mostly steep or vertical with intricate and active gullies)		

Recently, Sharma, H.S. (1968) in his valuable work on the Lower Chambal Valley has classified ravines on the basis of their width, depth and slope of side and head scarp into three grades as given in Table 5.2.

TABLE 5.2: Gully Classification (Sharma, H.S. 1968)

Particulars of ravines	Description of symbols of ravines		
	G_1	G_2	G_3
Depth in metres	Up to 1	1-5	5 up to 40
Bed width in metres	Up to 18	18-25	Above 25
Slope of head scarp	Gently sloping	Varies	Steep
Slope of sub-scarp	45°-80°	50°-90°	50°-90° but mostly vertical

FACTORS AFFECTING RAVINE EROSION

The overall factors affecting ravine erosion are climate, topography, rock type, vegetation, nature of streams, soil character and the upliftment process which has to be left open for additional factors, such as human interference which may be significant at a particular site.

Climatic Factor

The major climatic factors which influence run-off and erosion is precipitation. Precipitation is by far the most important. The erosion caused by rain is determined by the amount, intensity, and duration of the rainfall. For example, a short monsoon period, when the intensity of the rainfall is the highest. In the district the maximum intensity of rainfall (22 mm) is received within a span of three months. On the contrary, the remaining months have only 5 mm intensity. Hence, the ravines grow at a very fast rate during monsoon season.

The diurnal range of temperature is high in this district as it falls in the semi-arid climate. This temperature affects runoff by contributing to changes in soil moisture, causing cracks on the land surface during pre-monsoon.

Floods usually do not occur very frequently in the district. But plain areas along the Banas, the Morel and the Gambhir are relatively affected by flood hazard which cause effective ravine erosion in Boanli, Gangapur, Bamanwas tahsils.

Topographic Factors

The formation of ravines is highly affected by slopes. In Karauli, near Panchai river and between Manchi and Atta nadi where the slope ranges 5° to 6°, the gullies are more deeper and narrow, while in the north of Sri Mahaveerji where the slope decreases up to 3°, the ravines are shallow in depth. Though the slope does not affect gully initiation, yet it enhances headward and lateral extension of ravines. The bottom slope of the ravine is gentle which depicts a concavity in profile.

Structural or Rock Types

In this region gullying is more pronounced in those areas where solid geology is concealed by the thick soil or sediment cover. In Sawai Madhopur, Karauli and Khandar where Vindhyan Super Group is the main source of soil cover, it is highly liable to soil erosion. The worst ravines occur to the north and the east of Sawai Madhopur and Karauli tahsil.

The rocks of Aravalli Super Group, the shales, phyllites and quartzite yield heavier and more cohesive soils. Thus, in the south of Sawai Madhopur tahsil, Chauth-ka-Barwara and a long and narrow belt of Aravalli along western district boundary, the ravines are less pronounced.

Alluvium zone to the west of the hilly region, underlain by different geological strata, is second in order of degree of ravine and intensity.

Vegetation Factor

The forested slopes of the hills of Sawai Madhopur are relatively protected from soil erosion. Due to the mounting pressure of population and cutting of trees many forested areas are being converted into arable lands. Just below the Teli-ki-Panseri hills and near the Manchi hills, the whole low land area is severely chocked with ravine erosion. It is due to this that these hills are completely deforested. With the result it has accelerated gully erosion on pediment region. The field survey indicates that the ravines are developed on lowlands where the vegetation is scanty. During the monsoon torrential downpour through the cropless fields, the current fallows and the fallow lands are subject to erosion. The intensity of erosion being much higher in the later.

Soil Factor

The soils of the district are usually sandy loam to loamy in texture. The whole eastern and northern part is dominated by alluvial soils. It has been observed that the soils of this district are composed with 'Kankar Pan' and the percentage increases towards the sub-surface. With the climate and physiographic abnormalities in local environment the soils become more susceptible to ravine and gully erosion.

Forces Factor

Both the exogenic and endogenic processes affect soil erosion. The exogenic processes e.g. degradation in the upper parts of the slope and aggradation below imperceptibly alter the degree of slopes and the rates of soil erosion. The endogenic processes, like the dislocation along faults and change of levels involved in warping and tilting etc. may also affect ravine erosion to a small degree.

The study of long and cross profiles of the Banas and the Gambhir and its tributaries have shown some specific geomorphic features, such as incised meanders, slip off slopes, knick points which indicates the signs of neotectonism during Quarternary period. Thus the streams have been rejuvenated. To mention their courses the streams started to cut down the courses very fast and have made ravines more deep.

SHAPE AND SIZE OF RAVINES

In general, the depth of ravines ranges from 1 to 20 metres in the district. Only at a few places along the Panchai river and near the Chambal, this depth exceeds up to 24 metres. The depth of the ravines towards downstreams at the confluence of the Banas and the Chambal near Pali, increases considerably. Along the Chambal river, where small streams join it, the depth is above 20 metres. It is due to the thickness of the soil layer and the depth of the river channel. The author has found during a field study that, the depth of alluvium as well as the channel increase down stream. The average depth, the head scarp width and the bottom width of these ravines are 10 to 25 metres, 3 to 20 metres and 3 to 20 metres, respectively.

Generally, ravines of the district are 'V'-shaped or narrow 'V'-shaped. 'V'-shaped ravines are found where the subsoil is comparatively resistant to erosion than the top soil. The shape of ravines converts into 'U'-shape where thickness of alluvium increases. Such types of ravines are widespread near Hindaun, Jagar Tal, Panchai river and Machilpur.

GENESIS OF RAVINES

In the west a lot of work has been done concerning the origin of ravine like arrows, trenches, channels and bedlands. Some researchers correlate these features with climatic changes which causes modification to ground cover, concentration of run off and changes to the level of ground watertable. Others advocate that they are caused by human activities which have induced the concentration of surface flow (Hudson, 1971; Cooke, 1974; Patton and Schumm, 1975; Cooke and Reeves, 1976; Schumm, 1977; Graf, 1979).

In India, the explanation is given in landuse terms (Gupta, 1973; Gupta and Prajapati, 1983). Prajapati, 1982 and Ali, 1974, are of the opinion that gullies and ravines are the result of surface run-off mismanagement, especially, deforestation, overgrazing and ill-considered tillage in an environment which is particularly susceptible to erosion (Kaul, 1962; Tejwani, 1959). This susceptibility is, in part, due to the intensity and concentration of rainfall during the monsoon (Singh, *et al.*, 1976; Babu *et al.*, 1978; Raghunath *et al.*, 1982), and in part, due to the erodibility of the deep, alluvial soils where most of the ravines develop (Mehta, *et al.*, 1958; Verma and Patel, 1969; Narain *et al.*, 1979). Indiscriminate landuse practices and forest thinning are closely associated with ravine genesis (Sharma, 1980, p. 28).

Ravines are very rapidly developed erosional forms. They are usually not regarded as features of normal erosion but the result of changes in the environment, such as faulting, burning of vegetation, over-grazing, climatic change affecting vegetation, extreme storms, or any other cause of a break in vegetation which will bare the soil. Ravine erosion nearly always starts due to one of these two reasons: either there is an increase in the amount of flood runoff or the flood runoff remains the same but the capacity of water courses to carry the flood water is reduced.

In general, three popular theories have been introduced on the origin of ravine formation, which may be befitting for the area under study.

Over-grazing Theory

Bennett (1955), and Brice (1966) have advocated this theory. It is the soil that increases in run-off or the deterioration in channel stability which causes changes in vegetation cover especially the removal of trees, increase in the proportion of arable land in catchments, and excessive grazing which are the main factors responsible for ravine erosion. During the field study gullying was observed on the gentler or lower slopes of the scarps where the vegetation has been thinned or removed by men and livestock.

Climatic Theory

It was propounded by Antevs (1952), Schumm (1956), and Martin (1962). They take into account the change in climate accompanied by variations in rainfall periodicity and intensity. Gullying is a result of these seasonal changes in the climate where an aggradation occurs in the wet and degradation in the dry periods.

Upliftment or Rejuvenation Theory

The pioneer work on this theory has been done by Ahmad (1968) and Sharma (1976, 1980), they are of the opinion that the lowering of the local base level of erosion is caused by the upliftment of the region is the main cause of gully initiation. Recently Padmaja Rao (1976) in her study of Mej basin and Sharma (1980) in his study on 'The Morel and Chambal River Basins' have given very convincing attributes in favour of his theory.

The present area of study consists of the part of the Chambal, the Gambhir, the Banas and the Morel basins which are part and parcel of the aforesaid pioneer work. The Sawai Madhopur district lies at the juxtaposition of the older Aravallis to the newer Vindhyans.

There are several evidences like knick points in the form of waterfalls, incised meanders and slip off slopes, which supports the above explanation in the region under study.

STAGES OF RAVINE DEVELOPMENT

The mode of soil erosion by gullying or sheet erosion is not accurately known. There is a great shortage of quantitative studies of this aspect. Most of the accounts of soil erosion on the district, as a whole, are merely qualitative. According to Mr. Tejwani each ravine passes through a cycle of three stages which keeps repeating.

First Stage Rill Erosion

This consist of the cutting of a small channel or water course in the top soil, which, if unchecked, extends into sub-soil and small gullies are formed.

Second Stage Development of Ravine

The runoff water cuts deeper and deeper into sub-soil until it reaches the sand layers present in the lower depth. Once the sand layers are reached they are easily washed out and the top layers of soil and sub-soil topple down due to under-cutting and caving. This stage of gully development is characterised by vertical and caving gully heads.

Third Stage Stabilisation of the Ravine

During this stage the ravine readjusts itself to a stable horizon with relatively flat head and side slopes. Vegetation and shrubs establish rapidly on these mild slopes and make the gully stable till the whole cycle is repeated.

Further more, Sharma (1968, 1976, 1980) has given comprehensive elaboration of the various stages of the ravines in the lower Chambal Valley and the Morel Basin. The four stages ravine encroachment are as follow:

Swallow Hole Stage

With the initial action swallow holes take place along the river on the flat ground. It is a mutual action of rain water and the soil particles. The *Kankar* nodules in the Chambal region, in the district, provide more space to water to percolate in to the sub-soil.

Tunnelling Stage

At this stage the holes turn into tunnels like holes which are an important element in the headward extension of many ventical cuts. When water passes from the unravine floor of the swallow holes, it removes not only the salts in solution but also fine grained particles of soils from the base of the vertical ravine wall.

Collapsing Stage

At this stage, the fine particles and silts along with *Kankar Pan* move from their original place of deposition by the movement of water. The water accumulates in the voids formed by the above processes and accelerates the process of soil re-movement. Ultimately tunnels collapse from which a fulfledged ravine develops.

Recession Stage

The process of soil creep recedes the side scarps of the ravines. The weathered talus material accumulates at the base of the ravine scarps. With the continuous recession of the sides alluvial bluffs are disconnected or isolated. The collapsed material of the tunnel is subsequently removed by concentrated flow. Hence, the ravines enlarge their width and size. In the subsequent stage, the vegetation and shrubs establish rapidly on mild slopes and make the ravine stable till the whole cycle is repeated.

6

GEOMORPHIC REGIONS

ACCORDING TO Gellert (1982) , "geomorphic regionalisation involves the delimitation, characterisation and cartographic representation of general units of various rank and size orders." Geomorphic regions could be of immense value in planning and development, as various factors are taken into account while delineating these regions and units. The true potential of an area could be evaluated through minute investigation of geomorphic region and its units.

In the present study, a scheme of geomorphic regions of Sawai Madhopur district has been presented taking geological history and structure, lithological variations, slope, form of ground, quantitative properties of streams and surface morphology.

On these basis three major geomorphic regions with five sub-regions have been delineated, which are shown in Fig. 6.1.

The geomorphic units have different physical potentials and provide a sound base for rational landuse, soil and water conservation planning and development of the district.

1. The Hill System

   (A) The Aravalli Structural Hills

      (a) The Boanli-Bhagwatgarh Hills
      (b) The Lalsot-Bayana Hills

   (B) The Vindhyan Structural Hills

      (a) The Ranthambhor Plateau
      (b) The Sapotra-Karauli-Hindaun Hills
      (c) Inter-Mountain Valleys

2. The Dangland Plateau

   (A) The Valley Fills

3. The Lowland System

   (A) The Alluvial Plain
   (B) The Ravine Belt

FIG. 6.1

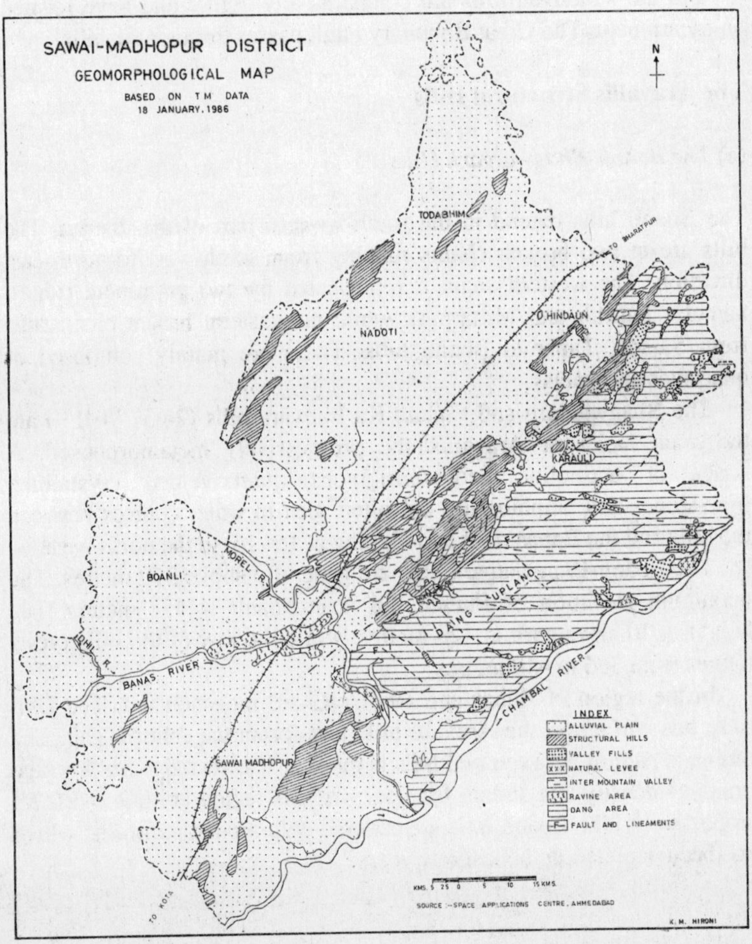

THE HILL SYSTEM

The Sawai Madhopur district lies on the eastern slope of the Aravalli ranges. The Aravallis are mainly found in the northern, western and southern parts which comprise Hindaun, Sawai Madhopur and Karauli sub-divisions. The south-west portion of the district comprises of low hills. In Karauli the hills are more pronounced and are composed of Vindhyan formations. The slope of the hills are gentle.

The main geomorphological characteristics of the Aravalli hills in the district, are highly dissected. They are usually flat topped with an average height of 240 to 360 metres.

But the Vindhyan hills are comparatively higher and have formed an escarpment. The Great Boundary Fault passes through the hills.

The Aravallis Structural Hills

(a) *The Boanli-Bhagwatgarh Hills*

The Boanli hills extend in the south-western part of the district. The hills are in two broken chains running from south-west to north-east direction. The western chain is represented by two prominent ridges, namely, Jamruli and Mittarpuri, while the eastern broken chain runs from Sarsop, Tapar to Boanli hills. These are mainly composed of quartzites and gneiss.

The Bhagwatgarh and Chauth-Ka-Barwara hills (26°3′, 76°13′) are the main facies of Aravallis and progressively metamorphosed. A series of actinolitic and ferruginous quartz-veined crystalline, lime-stones and amphibolites are often seen in water courses between the hills and the Banas river and dipping at 15°-16° to the north-west.

The Boanli-Bhagwatgarh hills are generally above 370 metres. The maximum elevation of Jhunun hill near Boanli is 452 metres. The height of Bhagwatgarh is 420 metres, while the rest of the hills crests ranges from 366 to 440 metres.

In the region of Banas and Dhil river are monsoon fed. The Dhil river has cut across the Aravalli hills and forms the Jamroli gap. The drainage pattern between two hills is more or less rectangular. Average drainage density and stream frequency of this region are 6-9 and 0.75, respectively. The Boanli hills are covered with moderate forests, which has been depleted in the last few years.

(b) *The Lalsot Bayana Hill*:

The Lalsot Bayana hills in the district enter from Toda Gurjar and from the district boundary line of Jaipur with Sawai Madhopur. Here, two off-shoots are visible. The hills are composed of the Alwar quartzites and pre-Aravalli gneiss. The arkose grits as well as quartzites are seen here. The base rocks are arkose, conglomerate, orthoquartzite. These pre-Cambrian rocks are worn downed by erosion into sharp serrate edges hills, and small ranges of low relative relief. Near Lewati (Bamanwas) these hills are widest with the highest peak of 527 metres. From here a narrow chain goes towards the north-east, and abruptly breaks at Moran Sagar. In Todabhim it again attains a good width and height of 439 metres. This hill system crosses Mahuwa and leads towards Bayana in the north-east.

The relief of this zone ranges from 200 to 220 metres and the slope value ranges between 4°-6°. At the foothills, scree materials has covered the slopes.

The drainage is interesting in many respects. The arrangement of quartzites and arkose has given rise to anticlinal ridges and synclinal valleys. Numerous rivers and rivulets originating from the unnamed peaks flow to the north-east and south-east and join the Gambhir and the Morel, respectively. Kareli nadi originates from Lalsot hills near Amarwas and takes its shape from Moran Sagar, ultimately making confluence with the morel in the south-east. Churhao river flows through Gudha narrow valley and coming down from Cherond hill joins the Gambhir at Nangal. The structural features further dominate the region and the trend of the flow of drainage is exactly in alignment with structural features. Upper Churhao Valley flow can be cited as an example of this trend. This region witnesses trellis drainage pattern in the south and the parallel in the north. Both are present between the two chains of the Aravallis. The average drainage density and stream frequency are comparatively lower than Boanli Hills, i.e., .6 and .5 respectively.

The Vindhyan Structural Hills

In the eastern part of the district, the entire Vindhyan succession is well developed. It extends from the south-west to the north-east, and leaves the district boundary towards Dholpur. Most of the structural hills occupy the western margins of the Dangland. In Sawai Madhopur tahsil the Vindhyan hills are intermingled with Delhi Super Group formations i.e., hematite shales and Gwalior's shales and Dolerites. After Banas Gap, further north the structural hills of Vindhyan System extends in the same direction. The hills are intersected with intermontane valleys, mostly consist of upper and lower Rewa sandstone, Jhiri and Panna shales. While the western outliers are composed of the Kaimur sandstone, conglomerate and Tirhon limestones. The main scattered hills are Lulloj and Dabra, Gothra and Simarda and Sonesri etc. The general height ranges between 300 and 420 metres. The topography of the area is highly rugged and undulating, this fact is verified from the serial of profiles (Fig. 6.2).

(a) *The Ranthambhor Plateau*

The fort of Ranthambhor stands at the centre in the south of Banas where the Gwalior system forms a syncline.

The Ranthambhor hills on the western margins, are composed of quartzite, interbedded with subordinate shales and dolerites flows or sills. The upper Vindhyans also occupy the significant position to the south-east of the Boundary Fault. The Vindhyans are mostly horizontal and form rounded mesas terminated by the steep scraps. At places the Vindhyans are inclined and form strike ridges.

The region consists of Ranwatzora Dungar (496 metres), Kalagarha (437 metres) south of Ranthambhor hill (506 metres) and north of it Khandar (501 metres), and Shampura (457 metres) ridges are chief representative peaks. The general height of the area from Mean Sea Level is 400 metres and represents the relicts of the pre-Cretacious-erosion surface. Structurally, to the north of Ranwatzora Dungar, the Ranthambhor hills rest upon the Gwalior Quartzite with intermittent hands of the Gwalior shales. The outer margins along the Chambal River look like an escarpment with the height of 180 metres.

Another peculiar structural feature of the area is the Boundary Fault which separates the Gwalior and Vindhyan System. The Great Boundary Fault is transacted with small local faults and Dhumar-Mal-ka-Darwaja Fault, Ranthambhor Fault and Undpura Fault. The central part of the Ranthambhor syncline from Kuchida to Baerdha village, bounded on each side by cliff of 15 metres, is a transverse valley fault. It is a good example of a rift valley.

The drainage seems to be influenced by the strike of the rocks, because on the western limb the hard rocks of dolerite and Gwalior shales influence the direction of streams for a short distance. The streams flow along the strike valley to the north-east into the Banas.

FIG. 6.2

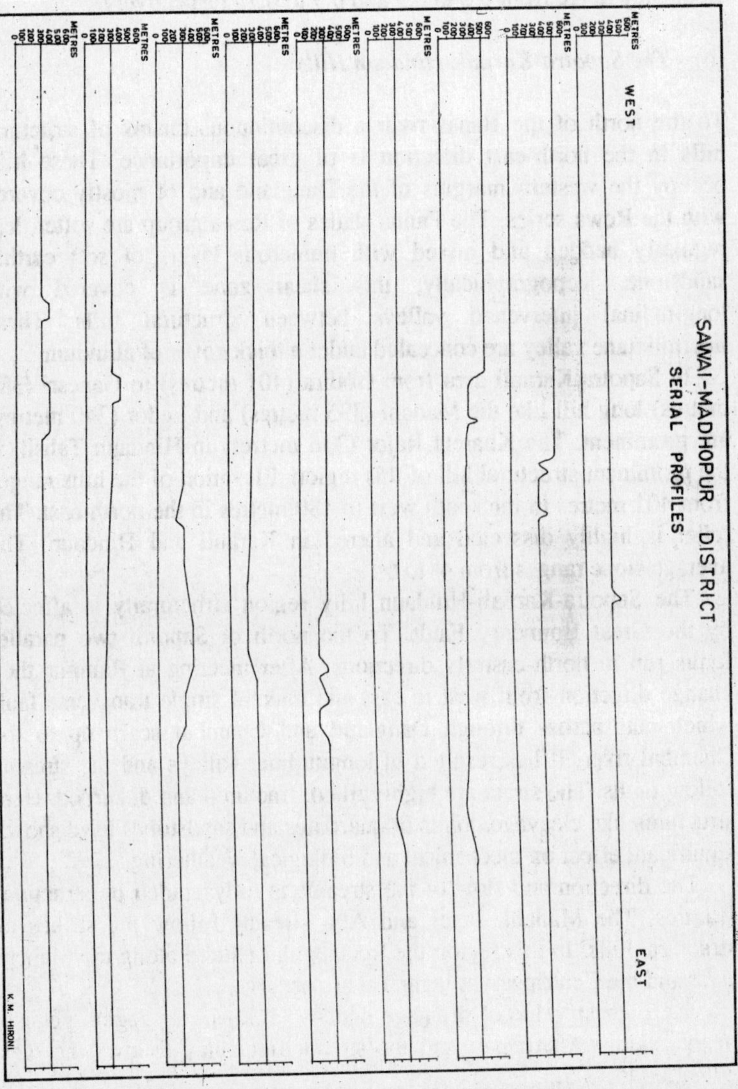
SAWAI-MADHOPUR DISTRICT
SERIAL PROFILES
WEST
EAST
METRES
K.M. HIRONI

The important river which runs along the strike line is Gambhir. The subsequent streams which descend from the south-eastern face of these hills directly join the Chambal at approximately right angle. Here, the drainage pattern is irregular. The average drainage density and stream frequency range from 0.6 to 0.9 and 0.5 to 0.75 respectively.

(b) *The Sapotra-Karauli-Hindaun Hills*

To the north of the Banas river a discontinuous chains of structural hills in the north-east direction is of great importance. These hills occupy the western margins of the Dangland and of mostly covered with the Rewa series. The Panna shales of Rewa group are softer, less regularly bedded and mixed with numerous layers of soft earthly sandstone. Topographically, this shear zone is covered with longitudinal intervened valleys between structural hills. These intermontane valley are concealed under a thick cover of alluvium.

In Sapotra-Karauli area from Gothra (401 metres) to Ganesri (380 metres) long hill like the Manchi (395 metres) and Ledor (340 metres) are prominent. The Khareta Rajor (336 metres) in Hindaun Tahsil, is the prominent structural hill of this region. Elevation of the hills ranges from 401 metres in the south west to 180 metres in the north-east. The relief is highly dissected and altered in Karauli and Hindaun. The average slope ranges from 4° to 6°.

The Sapotra-Karauli-Hindaun hilly region structurally is affected by the Great Boundary Fault. To the north of Sapotra two parallel faults run in north-easterly directions. After meeting at Rampur they change direction from west to east and make a single transverse fault which cuts across through Dangland and Chambal scarp up to the Chambal river. It has resulted in longitudinal valleys and the streams follow faults. The strata are highly tilted, fractured and disturbed. Here structures like cleavage, joints in quartzites and sandstones have shown significant effect on mechanical and biological weathering.

The direction and flow of the streams is fully guided by structural features. The Manchi, Jagar and Alta streams follow the strikes of structural hills. In this region the Rectangular pattern along the Manchi river and the Centripetal at Jagar Tal are observed.

The highest value of drainage density (1.32) in the region persists in the south-western part and the stream frequency follows the rank with 1.00 to 1.25.

(c) *Inter-Montane Valleys*

The underlying geological features of these inter-montane valleys are the same as these of the Sapotra-Karauli-Hindaun hills. These valleys consist of the lower Vindhyans. The inter-montane valleys almost run parallel and between the structural hills of the abovementioned region. The valleys are filled with sediments and gravels brought from the Jhiri and Panna shales of the Rewa group, sandstones of the upper Rewa and Kaimur group, the Tirhon limestone and conglomerates of the Semri group. In the north-east the Intermontane valleys are prominent with the sedimentary materials of the upper Bhandar sandstones and shales.

Inter-montane valley region, structurally is a weaker zone. The faulted topography of the area is concealed under a thick cover of colluvium. The streams within the region have formed this unit which is covered with fine debris. Near the hill the depth of the colluvium is low. The slope angle of this unit varies from 95 metres in the south-west to five metres in the north-east.

The boundary of these inter-montane valleys on the south is marked by Namada and Haroti near the Morel river. On the north-east it enters in Bayana near the Tali protected forest. Three inter-montane valleys are observed within the region. The first long valley extending for about 32 kilometres from Nimoda to the east of Wazirpur between the Lulluj, Mohanpur and the Gothra, Goneseri hills. The second valley extends from Gothra to Karauli parallel to the first Nimoda-Wazirpur valley lying between the Gothra-Goneseri and the Dangland. It is disconnected at some places. The Garana, Bariya and Makanpur are the main inter-montane valleys of the Gothra-Karauli region. The third valley is the Karauli-Hindaun inter-montane valley. The representative valleys are Chainpur between Manchi and Chhawar hills and the Machilpur valley between Fatehpur and Gubrenda hills in Karauli tahsil. The Jagar valley extends between Karesi and Khareta Rajor hills in Hindaun tahsil.

Since the valleys are long and narrow, therefore, they have an irregular drainage pattern. The trellis pattern is the most common because rills and fingertips run down and join at right angle with the main stream. The drainage density and stream frequency are high ranging from .6-.9 and 0.75 to 1.00 respectively. All the streams are mainly structurally controlled.

THE DANGLAND PLATEAU

The hill system in the south-east abruptly becomes less prominent to the north-east of the Banas water gap. From here it runs through the Karauli sub-division and merges into the Yamuna. The name has been given after the local term as 'Dang', which specifies a rugged region. This geomorphic region is highly denuded and dissected part of the district.

The Dangland is a landscape dominated by the upper Bhandar sandstone. Its eastern margins along the Chambal river consists of the Sirbu shales and the Bhandar limestones. To the north-west it is bounded by the Karauli hills along the Boundary Fault. Here, the Upper Bhandar Sandstone merges into the alluvium plains of Hindaun.

On the eastern margins of Dangland up to Dholpur, the Upper Bhandar limestone and Sirbu shales mark a long dissected wall like scrap extending for a length of nearly 112 kilometres from the Banas water gap, parallel to the Chambal river. It has been shown in Fig. 6.1 with a fault line. Chatterjee and Bagchi (1957) hold that the Chambal scarp is a fault scarp and it defies any explanation provided by fluvial morphology. But Sharma, H.S. (1980), advocates that the scarp is not the result of faulting but is a scarp resulted by fluvial action.

The structure of the Dangland is very simple. Broad Dangland terminated by vertical scarps, where the sandstone formations are horizontal. Strike ridges are common where these formations are dipping. Two parallel faults pass through the Dangland. The westerly fault from Haroti to Gurdeh hills and the easterly fault, from Barel (Jagir) to Dhamoniya Khon hills, are extending in the north-east direction in the district. These parallel faults are interrupted at several places (about 11 places) by the local transverse faults, which are probably disassociated with the main tectonic movements (Heron, 1922).

The elevation of this geomorphic region varies from 476 metres (The Utagir ridge) on the southern edge and towards the north-west it decreases to 300 metres. The streams of the area have eroded and dissected the surface into flat topped mesas. Besides this, many longitudinal valleys are in the regions of Sirbu shales. The eroded mesas of the Dangland are the representatives remanents of the Middle Miocene period (Sharma, 1979).

The Dangland plays a vital role in the drainage system of the area. It is a water shed between the Banganga and the Chambal systems. The numerous small streams descend from the eastern and southern edges have carved out the scarp desperately. The Manchi, Atta and Panchna tributaries that form the Gambhir, come down from the plateau and flow towards the north-west. They have dissected the area into bedland topography. Most of the streams of the region follow the slope trend and display a network of dendritic drainage pattern. Being a highly dissected topography, the highest drainage density value (1.32) are observed in the south-west and central Dangland, decreasing up to .3 in the north-west. The same pattern is followed by stream frequency with highest values in the south-west and which decreases up to 0.25 in the north-west.

The Valley Fills

This region lies between the scarp and the Chambal river and the north and the north-west of the Dangland. The valley fills are in different pockets scattered over the Dangland. Geologically, in the east, the valleys are filled with the upper Bhandar limestone and Sirbu shales sediment brought by the streams descending from the scarp. The Sirbu shales are characteristically dark red to olive in colour and easily erodable. The medium black and greyish soils of the valleys verify the fact. The north and the north-western valley fills are strictly dominated by the upper Bhandar sandstone underlain by shales.

These valley fills are comparatively plain areas. The general elevation in the east on the base of the scarp varies from 180 metres to 220 metres. The main valley fills of the eastern part are the Chandelipur, Durgawan, Mandrael, Rodhain and Karanpur, while in the north and the north-west the elevation of the valley fills ranges from 200 metres to 240 metres. Khunda, Machilpur, Chilbura and Tamangarh in the north-west and Chainpur, Khera and Chhawar are the main valley fills in the north.

THE LOWLAND SYSTEM

The vast monotonously flat to gently undulating, lowland system of the district, covers Mahwa, Todabhim, Bamanwas, Gangapur, Boanli and a considerable area of Hindaun, Sawai Madhopur and Karauli tahsils. The lowland system may be divided into three micro-geomorphic regions, namely, the alluvial plains, the ravine belt and the natural levees region.

The Alluvial Plain

This largest area of the district is covered by recent and sub-recent deposits. A broad expanse of alluvial plain of rivers Uttangan, Chambal, Banas, Morel and Gambhir which were deposited in the Pleistocene cycle of erosion. But now these rivers are being actively engaged in under-cutting their own deposited sediments. Since the Plain is bounded with the Aravallis in the west and the Vindhyan in the east, therefore, its source of alluvium has been the two system. In the north the upper Bhandar sandstone rocks are deeply concealed under the thick cover of this riverine alluvium brought by the streams descending down from the Vindhyan formations. While in south and south-west and west, the alluvium is underlain with the Delhi Super Group and the Aravallis rocks.

This region has a natural gradient to the east which is obvious from the natural flow of the Banas, the Morel, the Churhao and the Banganga rivers. Only the Chambal and the Gambhir flow from the south-west to the north-east. The plain varies in elevation from about 206 metres above Mean Sea level in the central part of 262 metres in the east and the west. But in the south-east along the Chambal it decreases up to 180 metres.

The Geomorphological Map (Fig. 6.1) shows, the alluvial plain in the south-east of Sawai Madhopur-Ranthambhor hills, is actually the south-eastern extension of the vast region of sediments stretching from west of Sawai Madhopur to Mahwa tahsils. This is a plain region of smaller tension along the Chambal river. The several tributaries of the Chambal viz., Chaken and Kundi nadi flows through this region. This plain extends up to Barel Jagir (Khandar) across the Banas.

In this monotonous plain some ridges and hillocks, usually of the Aravallis and the Delhi Super Groups provide some change of relief. Bhagawatgarh (420 metres), Boanli (451 metres) and Lewali (526 metres) are the prominent hills.

The infill landscape is developed in narrow bands mainly along the two sides of the Banas and the Morel. It is a zone of intense alluviation. A noteworthy feature of the whole area is that it has an annual renewal of its fertility and productivity by fresh deposition of sand, silt and clay. There are only a few permanent streams viz. the Banas and the Morel but ephemeral channels are numerous. The waters of the south and the north of the Banas are collected by Galwa, Gambhir and Dhil nadi, whereas the water of the northern part of the Morel is collected by Karsil and Kareli.

The larger streams exist with the dendritic drainage pattern, while the radial patterns are observed on domal structures of the Aravallis. The drainage lines are lesser on the west. But the confluence point of the Banas and the Morel, has the highest drainage density (1.00) and stream frequency (1.22). The slope value is also the lowest up to 2°. To the north and the north-west, the upper Bhandar sandstone and recent deposits stretches from the Moran Sagar and Udai Sagarline to the northern most tip of the district across the Utangan river. The plain forms monotonous tract except intersected by the Alwar series (422 metres) in Todabhim and undulating in nature towards the east and north-east due to the Main Boundary Fault that passes through this region.

Relief elevation ranges from 180 metres in the west to 166 metres in the east. The slope value is the lowest and ranges from 0° to 2°.

The flatness of the area bears the highest agricultural value. It does not allow the expansion and bifurcation of streams into smaller channels and thus the larger streams exist with the dendritic drainage pattern. The Utangan river flows west to east through Mahwa. It does not form any regular drainage pattern. The stream frequency is the lowest being below 0.25 and the drainage density is below 0.03 in the region.

The Ravine Belt

Almost all the streams of this region show intense gullying and ravine erosion. Most of the ravines are concentrated in the longitudinal intervened valleys carved out on the Dangland. Here the Vindhyan sandstone, shale and quartzites are most vulnerable to ravine erosion. The horizontal beds of the Vindhyan Super Group form a level table surrounded by bold vertical cliffs, from where the swift flowing small rills and finger tip streams descend down and cut the easily erodable crumbling shales in the region. Beside this the recent and sub-recent alluvium is also common for intense ravine erosion.

As already stated in the previous chapter of the ravine morphology, the three ravined areas are observed in the district, i.e., the Gambhir-Panchai-Manchi area, the Banas-Chambal confluenced area and the Morel-Banas ravined area. The intensity of ravine erosion seems to increase as one proceeds downstream along all the rivers.

The elevation of ravine areas differ from place to place. In the Gambhir-Manchi area, it is 240 metres to 260 metres, the Banas-Chambal 200 metres to 220 metres and in the Morel-Banas it is only 180 metres to 190 metres.

Being a highly dissected and denuded topography the highest drainage density prevails in the north-east of the Dangland and at the confluence of the Banas and the Morel ravine areas decreasing up to 0.3 to 0.6 in the north of the Morel and the Gambhir. Similarly, the stream frequency also shows the same pattern of existence with the highest value above 1.00 along the Banas-Morel confluence, decreasing below 0.25 in the north of the Gambhir and the Morel.

7

EXISTING LANDUSE

IN THE foregoing analysis in the previous chapters, various aspects of geomorphology have been discussed. It is beyond doubt that landuse and agriculture of any area is primarily dependent on the nature of landforms and their morphology. In this part an attempt is being made to analyse landuse changes and characteristics of the district in relation to geomorphology.

Activity on the land has been the major criterion for classifying landuse which is essentially a qualitative rather than a quantitative phenomenon. Since, land is a basic factor of production, and it is a continuing source of amazement, therefore, few have deemed it fit to adequately survey landuse. Without a system of monitoring landuse change, how can emerging trends be identified, how can cost be measured, policies formulated and action initiated to meet socially, economically and ecologically undesirable trends.

In the Sawai Madhopur district, the net area sown and the total cropped area have had a very meagre increase in a decade (1975-76 to 1985-86). It has increased from 4,77,200 hectares to 4,85,121 hectares and 5,69,150 hectares to 5,72,327 hectares respectively. On the contrary, there are some areas, specially ravine lands, where the use of land resources are still inadequate due to the lack of water supply, presence of ravines and ignorance of the cultivators. Consequently, there has been a decline in the double cropped area in the district i.e. 91,950 hectares in 1975-76 and 87,206 hectares in 1985-86.

The present chapter proposes to examine the general and existing landuse pattern of the Sawai Madhopur district keeping the above facts in mind. Landuse statistics for the period 1976 to 1986 have been taken from the publications of the Directorate of Economics and Statistics, Rajasthan, Jaipur and other Tables of Agricultural Statistics of Sawai

Madhopur district (1986) situated at Sawai Madhopur. Tahsil level statistics of eleven tahsils were used for analysing the distributional patterns of general landuse. An attempt is also made to examine changes that have occurred during a span of a decade i.e. from 1975-76 to 1985-86.

LAND CLASSIFICATION

The census of India have classified land utilisation in nine different categories but in the present study these have been grouped into major landuse categories, as the percentage of area under individual categories is relatively insignificant. Table 7.1 (1985-86) brings out the main elements of land utilisation in the Sawai Madhopur district.

TABLE 7.1: Landuse in Sawai Madhopur District (1985-86)

Sl. No.	Major Landuse Categories	Area in hectares	Percentage of total geographical area
1.	Forest	2,37,025	22.50
2..	Not available for cultivation	1,67,123	15.84
3.	Other uncultivated (excluding fallow land)	99,473	9.44
4.	Fallow land	65,654	6.22
5.	Net Area Sown	4,85,121	46.00
	Total	10,54,396	100.00

The total geographical area of the district is 10,54,396 hectares. Table 7.1 and Appendix IX depict the general landuse categories both at the district as well as the tahsils level (1985-86). The salient features which are discernible in the intra-regional variations may be identified as follows:

1. Forested land is more in the north-east, the east and the south-east (Sawai Madhopur district) than in the south-west, west and north-west and occupies significant proportions of the uplands of the Vindhyans and Aravallis.
2. The area of the barren and uncultivated land is significant in hilly tracts, ravines, stony waste and sandy lands. Broadly speaking it lies in the north-eastern part, the north-west of Boanli, along the Banganga river, and in some pockets of

Nadoti and Gangapur and the Danglands.

3. The extent of land put to non-agricultural uses is high in the south-east, north-east of Karauli, south of Gangapur and slopes of Aravallis in Bamanwas and Nadoti. Here grasslands and grass scrubs are dominant due to lack of irrigation and underground water being on piedmont regions.
4. The proportion of fallows is also high all over the west and the south-west of district, as the irrigation facilities are limited and the rainfall, too, is scanty and confined to the south-west monsoon season alone.
5. The net area sown is confined to fertile lowlands lying in the north and the west and the uplands with relatively good soil cover.

A detailed analysis of landuse in Sawai Madhopur district comprising the eleven tahsils using averages for 10 years from 1975-76 to 1985-86 has been attempted

Forest Land

This category includes all areas under forests under any legal enactment dealing with the forests. The forests of the district are classified into three major categories — reserved, protected and unclassed forests (Fig. 7.1).

Most of the dense forests are situated on the main exposures of Bhandar, Rewa and Kaimur groups of the Vindhyan system. These dense forests are rooted on hills of sandstone, limestone and shales. In the eastern part of the district Ranthambhor, Khanoar, Khandar, Marmda, Chirnulkho Kased, Chhawar and Neola are the main densed forests and consist of the famous game sanctuary of Ranthambhor. The trees of these areas are *Dhok (Anogeissus pendula), Raunj (Acacia leucophloea), Tendu (Diaospyres-melanoxylon), Bamboo (Dhandrocalamus Btrictus)* etc. In the south, other dense forests are confined to the deep rich soils on the outcrops of Gwalior dolerites in Sawai Madhopur hills which mostly run along the bottoms of deep narrow valleys. The chief species comprise Chola, Bor and Guter.

In the western and the south-western parts of the district, some scattered dense forest patches are on Alwar and Gwalior system of the Aravallis. Moran Dungar, Rewal, Boanli and Bhagawatgarh are the representative forest areas.

FIG. 7.1

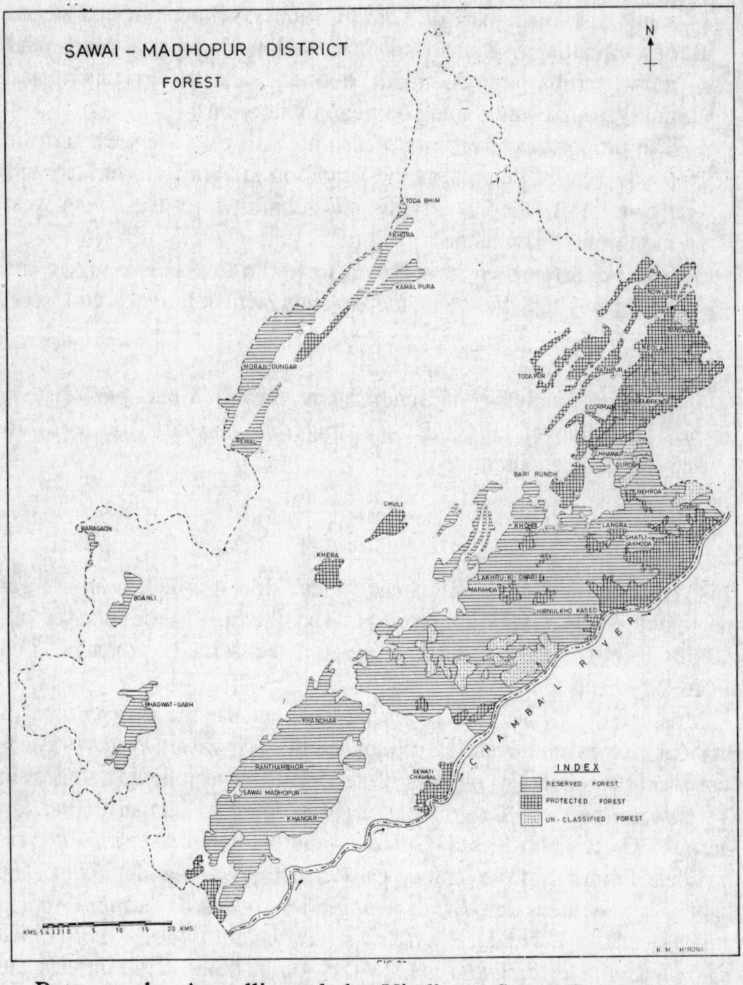

Between the Aravallis and the Vindhyan Super Groups, the low land areas comprising Mahwa, Todabhim, Hindaun, Gangapur, Bamanwas and Boanli tahsil are generally devoid of forest cover. Hence, the level land has been either entirely brought under the plough or under the pastures.

The forests occupy about 22.5 per cent of the total geographical area in Sawai Madhopur, being higher than the average for Rajasthan which is about seven per cent. The density of forests is not uniform everywhere as there are marked variations in their regional distribution at the tahsil level. The data of 1975-76 and Fig. 7.2 reveal that the percentage of forest ranges from under four per cent in Hindaun (2.34%), Mahwa (2.09%), Gangapur (3.25%) and Boanli (2.55%) to over 40 per cent in the north-east and the east. This highest percentage is recorded in Sapotra (35.71%) and Karauli (36.8%). In other parts of the Nadoti and Sawai Madhopur tahsils, forest occupy between 13 to 20 per cent of the total geographical area of the tahsil.

FIG. 7.2

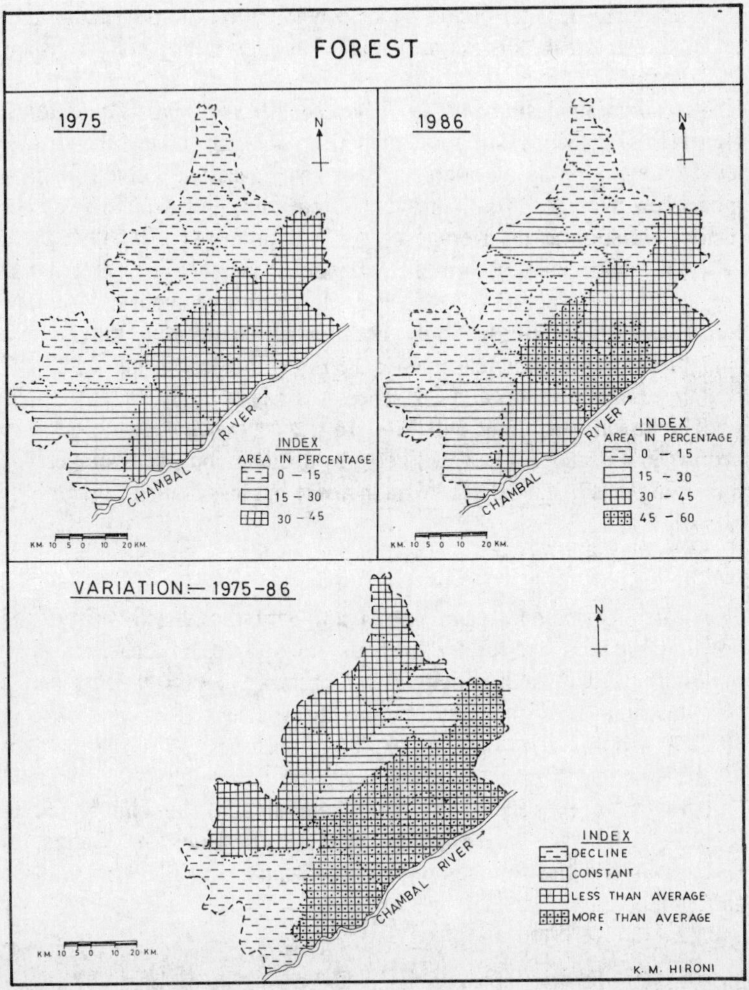

The percentage of forest areas in 1985-86 (Appendix XI) has increased in a number of tahsils of the district. According to these statistics of 1985-86 the tahsils of Sapotra (52.1%), Karauli (40.60%) and Khandar (34.79%) have tremendously high percentage of area under forest. The tahsils of Sawai Madhopur (19.69%) and Nadoti (15%) have percentage of forest area between 15 per cent to 20 per cent. Remaining tahsils like Boanli (3.75%), Gangapur (3.25%), Hindaun (2.34%) and Mahwa (2.6 per cent) have very small area under forest. Figure 7.2 shows the regional distribution of forest area in the district.

During the decadal period under consideration the percentage area under forests for the district as a whole has grown only marginally i.e. 3.7 per cent.

A comparative study of 1975-76 and 1985-86 statistics of forest area is illustrated by variation map (Fig. 7.2), by taking the district level of variation as an average. Four categories are formed, namely more than average, less than average, constant and decline from the district variation as an average i.e. +3.7, Sapotra (+16.39%), Khandar (+6.67%) and have shown a tremendous increase i.e. more than average, while Karauli (+3.8%) has shown an average increase. The forest area has increased only because of changes in the landuse categories. The area increase under the forest in above tahsils is 23,727 hectares, 6,498 hectares and 6,926 hectares, respectively.

The Sawai Madhopur tahsil (–1.16 per cent) has shown a trend to decline in a decade. It is 1,958 hectares decline from the average. The remaining tahsils have depicted an increase but less than the average.

Land not Available for Cultivation

This category includes land put to non-agricultural use, barren and unculturable land like hills, river beds, ravine infested areas, railways, buildings etc. The landuse map (Fig. 7.3) shows that this type of land is well distributed in the district. The district has 18.32 per cent in 1975-76 and 15.84 per cent in 1985-86 of such land. A substantial part of the district is rugged being unfit for cultivation. The bedland topography of the Banas, Morel, Chambal and Gambhir rivers in Karauli, Khandar and Hindaun and sand dunes in Gangapur, Bamanwas and the Ranthambhor hills occupy land not available for cultivation.

FIG. 7.3

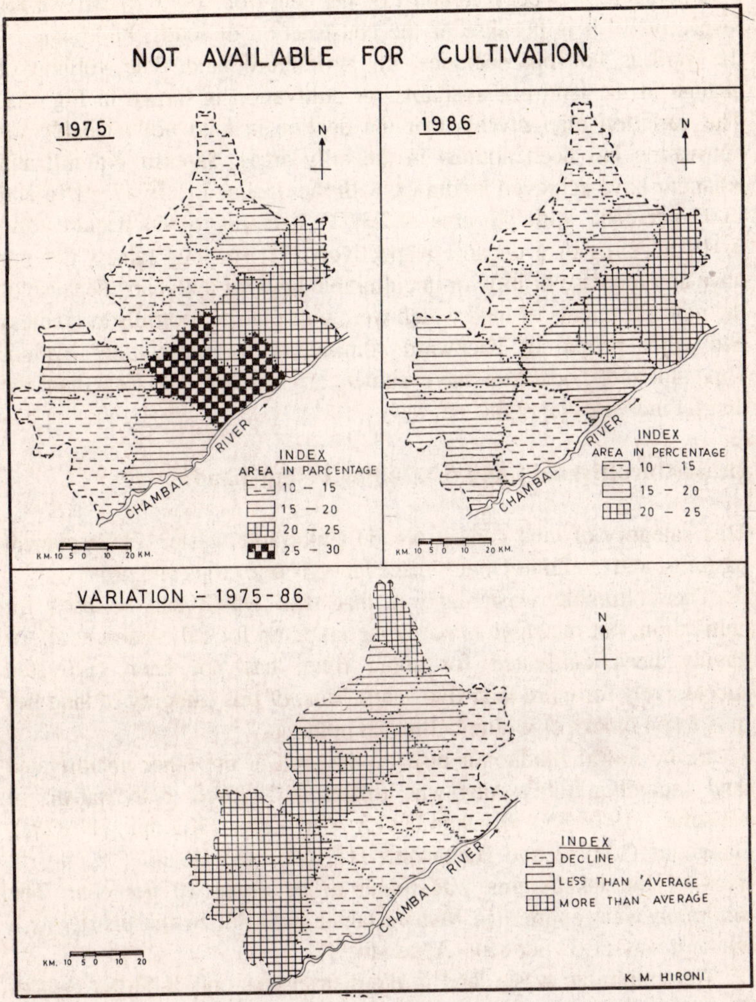

Figure 7.3 (1976 and 1986) shows that the maximum land not available for cultivation exists in the hilly tahsils, in the eastern parts of the district. In 1975-76 (Appendix X) the land under this category was the highest in Sapotra and Karauli i.e. 30.3 per cent and 24.17 per cent and in 1985-86 it decreased to 16.78 per cent and 20.43 per cent respectively. It is evident from the Appendices X and XI.

Sawai Madhopur, Gangapur and Boanli tahsils show an increase of 2.74 per cent, 2.79 per cent and 1.04 per cent from 1975-76 to 1985-86, respectively. It is because of the construction of roads, buildings, by the various housing societies, on agriculture land. The volume of change in the land not available for cultivation is shown in Fig. 7.3. The variation map reveals that the decline in land not available for cultivation has been noticed in the hilly areas. Sapotra, Karauli and Khandar have achieved landmark with the decline of -16.57, -3.74 and -3.07 per cent, with the area of 23,219 hectares, 6,764 hectares and 2,919 hectares in a decade, respectively. These three tahsils did not have any increase or hilly or unculturable land for ten years, because of the new allotments of land which were made in the foothills to landless and other people of backward community for cultivation. Nadoti, Hindaun and Todabhim have shown an increase but less than the district increases i.e. 2.48.

Other Uncultivated Land (Excluding Fallow Land)

This category of land consist of: (1) Culturable waste, (2) Permanent pastures, and (3) Land Under miscellaneous tree crops and groves.

The culturable waste land is that land which can be used for cultivation, but the same is not being taken up for cultivation at all, or having been cultivated for some time, has not been cultivated successively for more than five years. Most of this category of land lies in isolated blocks or within cultivated holdings.

In the Sawai Madhopur district, the area of the other uncultivated land excluding fallow land was greater in 1975-76 in the tahsils of Khandar (19.06%), Hindaun (14.8 per cent), Karauli (12.82%), Gangapur (13.6%) and Bamanwas (12.16%) and Boanli (12.3%). In most of the tahsils this was found to be about 10 per cent. The minimum was reported in Mahwa tahsil (6.48%). In the district as a whole it was 11.62 per cent (Appendix X).

The culturable waste land in the district was only 9.43 per cent of the arable land in 1985-86. However, the percentage of culturable waste land ranges from 5.41 to 14.06 per cent in the various tahsils of the district. Hindaun topped the list with 14.06 per cent, Karauli follows with 12.66 and Khandar 13.85 per cent. The lowest is in Mahwa (5.41%).

Figure 7.4 (1975-86) reveals that high percentage of culturable waste is found in the north-east, east, and south parts of the district and are covered with hills as such culturable waste land is found in the foot hills where efforts for better land utilisation are not economically feasible. In the eastern part the soils are calcareous dunal and many areas have adversely been affected by flood erosion and scarcity of water. Due to these negative factors this category of land has become uneconomic to cultivate.

FIG. 7.4

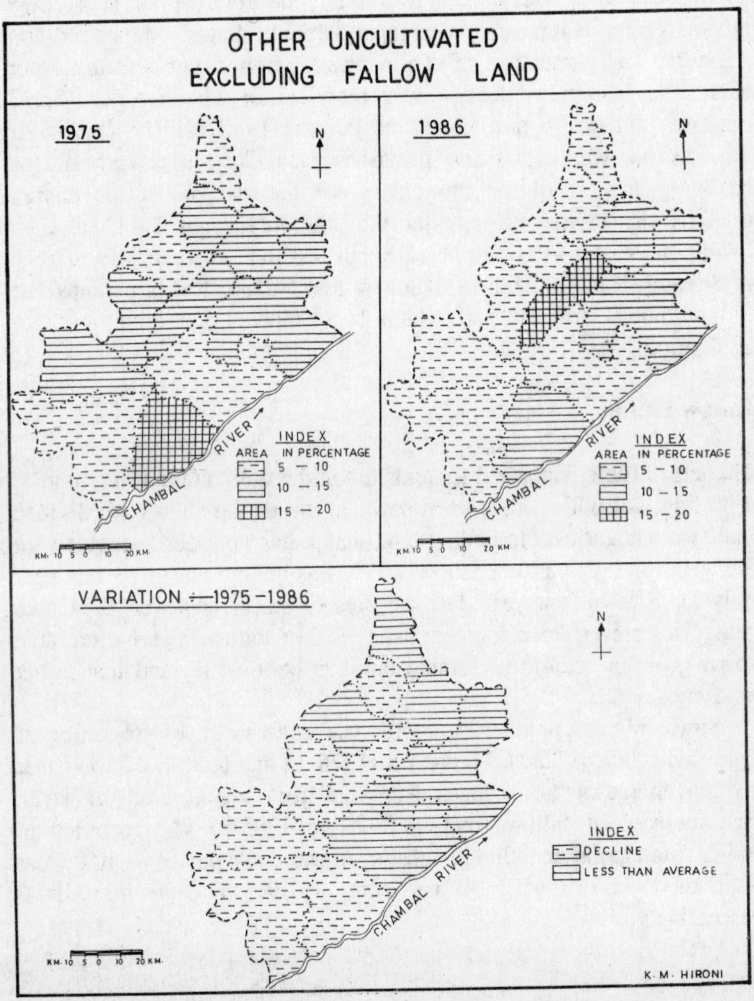

Permanent pastures and other grazing lands are earmarked in every village at the rate of 0.12 hectare per cattle head according to the settlement rules. The data for 1985-86 (Appendix IX) show that maximum pasture land was in Karauli and Khandar which was 14,549 hectares and 11,410 hectares respectively. The lowest pasture area in the Todabhim was reported as 2,869 hectares, because of less cattle population.

Figure 7.4 (variation map) shows the change of 10 years of other uncultivated land. It depicts an overall decline from the district average in Todabhim, Bamanwas, Gangapur, Boanli, Sawai Madhopur and Khandar. The percentage of decline ranges from 5 per cent to 15 per cent. The maximum decline was recorded in Khandar i.e. 18,273 hectares in 1975-76 and 13,316 hectares in 1985-86. The reason for this decline was either the provision of reclamation work or the changing attitude of the farmers in the eastern part of the district towards the ravine lands, after the introduction of Panchna Dam Irrigation Project. A slight increase, but less than average, was marked in Sapotra, Karauli, Mahwa, Hindaun and Nadoti. It was perhaps due to continuous soil erosion which has rendered the area unfit for cultivation.

Fallow Lands

The term fallow is applied to lands not under cultivation at the time of reporting, but which have been sown in the past. Fallows are divided into two categories. (1) Fallow land which has not been cultivated for 3-5 years and (2) Current fallow which was not cultivated for one year only i.e., the current year. For the present study, however, these two categories are grouped together. The total of fallow land and net area sown gives the extent of 'arable land' in contrast to land that is not cultivated at all.

Sawai Madhopur district records (i.e. 10% to 15%) proportion of land under fallow lands. Figure 7.5 (1975-76 and 1985-86) shows that the percentage of fallow lands decreased from west to east and north. The increase of fallow from 1975-76 to 1985-86 was recorded in Sawai Madhopur and Boanli tahsils. It was 5.65 per cent, 10.92 per cent in 1975-76 and 8.02 per cent, 13.59 per cent in 1985-86 respectively.

FIG. 7.5

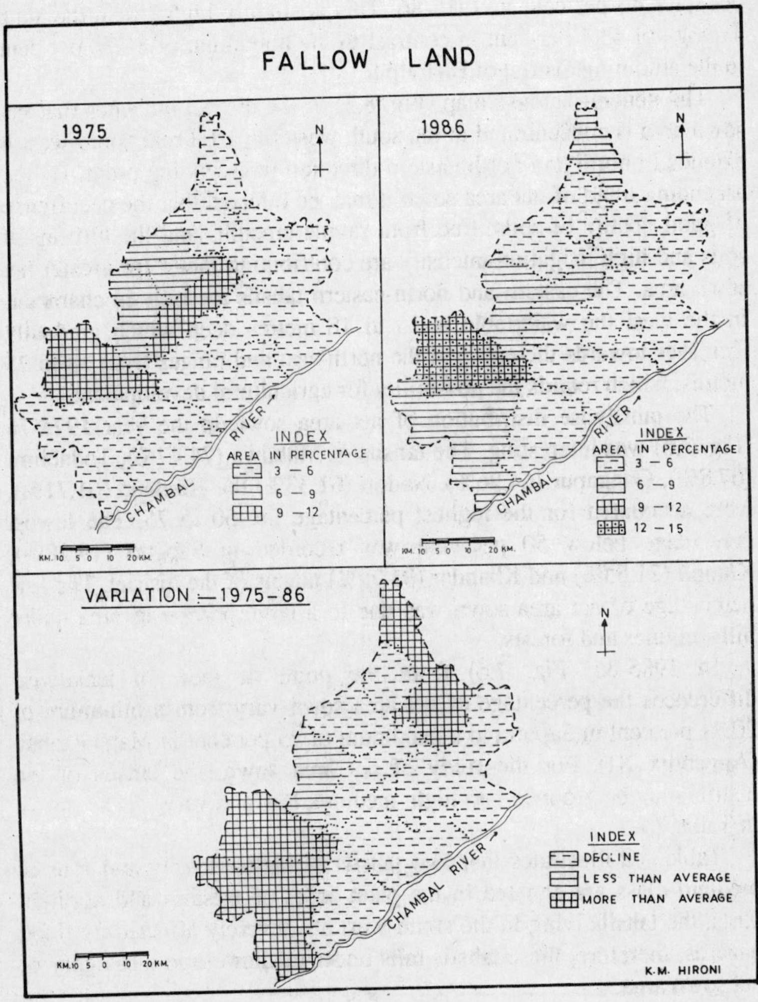

Figure 7.5. (variation map) illustrates a trend of decline from the district average (+0.25) in Khandar (-0.84), Gangapur (-0.46), Nadoti (-2.49) and Todabhim (-0.32), while Bamanwas has a slight increase but less than average.

Net Area Sown

The net area sown is the actual area under crops, double-cropping is

Doubled-cropped Area

This category of land represents the area on which crops are cultivated more than once during the agricultural year. In 1975-76 the area under double-cropping was very limited. Only on 91,950 hectares of land double cropping was practised. The maximum percentage of double cropped area to net sown area was found in Hindaun (28.24%), i.e. 18,068 hectares, Mahwa (25.62%) 12,250 hectares, Todabhim (25%) 12,000 hectares. In all the tahsils of the district, it was below 10 per cent. Khandar had the lowest percentage of double cropped area i.e. only 1.04 per cent (Fig. 7.7).

In 1985-86 the maximum percentage of double cropped area was found in Hindaun (28.00 per cent) followed by Mahwa (23.33 per cent) and Todabhim (22.22 per cent) (Fig. 7.7)

Figure 7.7 shows the variation of ten years from the district average (-0.45%). The Sawai Madhopur, Khandar, Karauli and Sapotra tahsils have shown increase of area over the district average. Sapotra has increased double cropping area tremendously i.e. from 3,286 hectares in 1975-76 to 7,411 hectares in 1985-86. While Hindaun has marked slight increase in the decade. This expansion of double cropped area is due to availability of water for irrigation, provision of manures and nature of crops which the farmers intend to grow.

Bamanwas, Todabhim and Nadoti have shown decline over district average. It is to some extent due to the non-profitable nature of farming, decline of soil fertility, low rainfall inadequate irrigation facilities, and negligence of ignorant farmers towards the intensification of agriculture.

Total Cropped Area

The large parts of the district are level, owing recent and sub-recent alluvial soils. Sub-recent areas are undulating or rolling in nature. 54.26 per cent of the total geographical area is under cropped land which is discernable from Appendix XI.

From the point of view of tahsilwise differences the percentage of total cropped land vary from a minimum of 25.85 per cent in Sapotra to a maximum of 98.00 per cent in Mahwa tahsil (Appendix XI). For the study of total cropped land, the tahsils of the district may be grouped into high, medium, low and very low.

Table 7.3 reveals that three tahsils fall under high intensity and two under medium intensity, which mostly lie in the northern and western plains of the district. The tahsils lying in the southern and eastern hilly parts belong to low and very low percentage groups.

FIG. 7.7

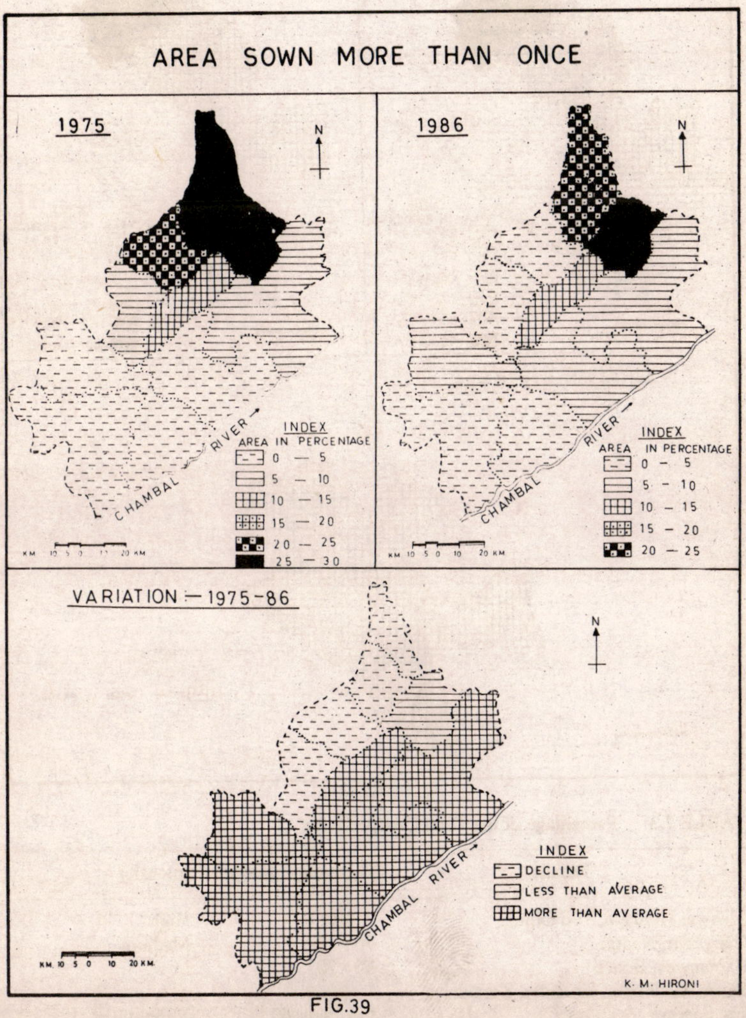

FIG.39

FIG. 7.8

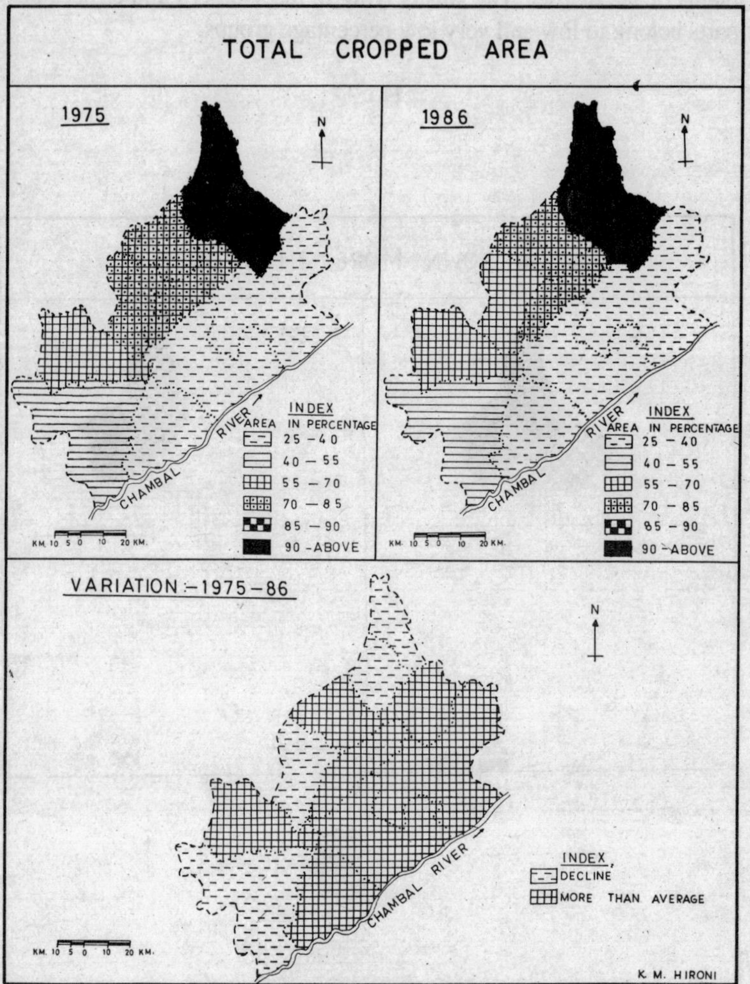

FIG. 40

TABLE 7.3: Percentage of the Total Cropped Area

Tahsils	Percentage groups	Intensity
Mahwa, Hindaun, Todabhim	Above 80	High
Gangapur, Nadoti	70 - 80	Medium
Bamanwas, Boanli	60 - 70	Low
Sawai Madhopur, Khandar, Karauli and Sapotra	Less than 60	Very low

The tahsilwise distribution of the total cropped area in the year 1975-76 (Fig. 7.8) is clear from Appendix X. The tahsils of Mahwa (100.8%), Hindaun (90.79%), Todabhim (93.42%), Gangapur (75.75%), Nadoti (70.75%), Bamanwas (72.29%) had shown high total cropped area in 1985-86. The tahsils of Mahwa (98.00%), Hindaun (92.62%) and Todabhim (92.59%) have high percentage of the total cropped area. The tahsils of Sapotra (25.85%), Karauli (28.9%) and Khandar (35.41%) have shown slight increase and represent low intensity group.

During the period from 1975-76 to 1985-86, the percentage of the total cropped area clearly indicates the stable conditions of agriculture in the district, only 0.36 per cent area was added in the total.

Figure 7.8 (variation map) shows the changes in the total cropped area within 10 years. It reveals an overall decline from the district average (+0.36%) in Mahwa, Todabhim, Bamanwas and Sawai Madhopur. The maximum decline was recorded in Mahwa i.e. 1,835 hectares in the decade 1975-76 to 1985-86 (Appendices VIII and IX). The reasons for this decline are increase in the settlements, roads, and net sown area. A slight increase is marked in Sapotra, Karauli, Hindaun, Nadoti, Gangapur and Khandar, etc. It is perhaps decrease in *usar* and land under water bodies. During the field survey it was observed that the beds of the Banas, Gambhir have been brought under plough for raising summer crops

8

GEOMORPHOLOGY AND LANDUSE

THE AGRICULTURAL landuse pattern, indeed, is the result of interaction of geomorphic and historico-socio-economic factors. In Sawai Madhopur district the influence of geomorphic features on agricultural landuse has been investigated and presented. Since land utilisation in relation to geomorphology, particularly in semi-arid environment, has received scanty attention of the investigators. However, the valuable work in this direction has been done in Poland under the leadership of Professor Klimaszewski (1982). This study illustrates a method comparison of geomorphological maps and geomorphological evaluation maps with necessary explanatory text to the Kasokov region. The Division of the landuse Research, CSIRO, of Australia and Cooke et. al. (1974) have also contributed a lot in the similar direction.

In India Iyer and Srinivasan (1977), Sen and Singh (1977), Ghosh and Singh (1965), Subramanyan (1978), Vats and Singh (1982, 1983 and 1986), R.K. Rai, S.N. Patnaik, P. Panda and V. Singhania (1984), Vaidyanadhan (1980, 1984), D.K. Painuli (1984), Dutt, G.K. (1985) studied the landuse in relation to landforms.

SLOPE SUITABILITY AND AGRICULTURE

The effect of slope on agricultural landuse may be considered as direct. The most obvious direct impact of slope on agriculture is the limitations imposed on cultivation; while the indirect effects of slope are pedological and climatic, including the position of watertable, development of soil and drainage. For examining undulating terrain for planned cultivation the dynamism of the slope development and the relief (Fig. 8.1) must be considered.

FIG. 8.1

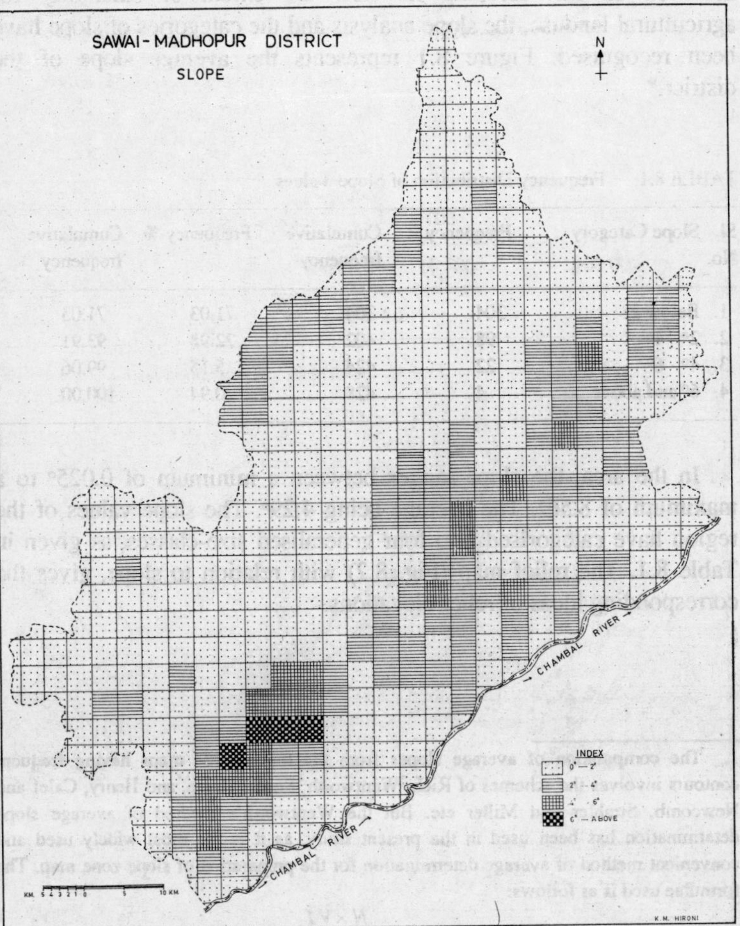

FIG. 41

In the district under investigation gentle slope ranging between 2° and 4° and a moderate slope from 4° to 6° are suggested to show suitability for annual and seasonal cropping respectively. With assured water supply the slope even up to 7° can be used for seasonal cropping and permanent pastures. The slopes of over 7° are usually covered by natural forests. With increasing slope angle, there is an increase in the slope instability, and hence it is essential to understand the relationship between the slope and the landuse category. A successful balance

Level Slope of Low Land Plains (below 2°)

Level slope of low land plains are encountered in Mahwa, Todabhim, Hindaun, Gangapur, Bamanwas, Boanli and South Western Sawai Madhopur tahsils occupying an area of about 7,600 sq km (71.03%) of the total area of Sawai Madhopur district. Most of this lies in the recent and sub-recent alluvial plains. This level surface of the great flat is caused by fluvial erosion and shows the penultimate stage of the cycle of erosion. The average height of this category is 210 metres. The occurrence of this type of slope, along the confluence points of the major rivers and streams, is rather natural because the area is affected by two strong denuding powers. In addition, small pockets of the category of slope are also observed in the intermontane valleys of the Dangland and Valley fills between the scarp and the Chambal river. It has been observed that such plains areas are devoted to such crops which protect against water erosion, namely, barley and wheat. These are ploughed twice a year for seasonal crops. About 26 per cent of the total net area sown in the district is occupied by this category. There are some problematic areas where the problem of salinity is present. Further, there is ample scope here for bringing more such saline land under cultivation.

Gentle Slope Zone (2°-4°)

A considerable portion of the plain region of the district i.e., 2,450 sq km (22.89%), is covered by this zone. It covers the major portions of Todabhim, Mahwa, Bamanwas and Karauli tahsils. This slope zone presents to some extent in Gangapur and Sawai Madhopur. In the west along the district boundary with Jaipur up to Mahwa and the central, the central-eastern and the south-western parts of the district, are under this category. The extension of this category is up to 280 metres. The gentle slope zone is most productive from the farming point of view provided there is a good supply of water. These fields are located along the gently slopping valley bottoms. About 16 per cent of the net sown area of the district is in this category. Some patches are suffering from salinity and alkanity, and the wasteland areas are prone to undulation which are problematic areas in this category.

Foothills of Moderate Inclination (4°-6°)

The slope zone of 4°-6° covers an area of 550 sq km (5.41%) of the total and occurs positively in the Dangland and the south and the central parts of the district. In the extreme south this slope zone is on the alluvial plain in the form of ridges; but in the north and the north-east the Gwalior shales and quartzites are the main rock hills. The general elevation of this category varies from 280 metres to 380 metres. It covers Sawai Madhopur, Khandar, Sapotra and Karauli tahsils.

The land put to cultivation of this slope is only 2.85 per cent. But the zone is equally significant. During the field traverse it was found that the scattered cultivation was taken up on the lower slopes of ridges. Their length is often 3 to 4 times that of their width. There is a direct relationship between their width and the gradient of the slope. It is, therefore, interesting to note that the lower the relative relief, the gentler is the slope and more significant is the agricultural potentiality of the areas.

Hills of Moderately Steep Inclination (6°-8°)

The highest slope angles (6°-8°) are observed in the south around Ranthambhor and hills of Khandar tahsil and it covers an area of 100 sq km (0.94%) of the total. The general height of this slope zone is above 400 metres. In this area, it is quite impossible to cut terraces for crop cultivation. Moreover, climatic and soil conditions are too harsh for agronomic practices. Despite this fact some area of this category has been found under cultivation which is mainly confined to valleys, and protected places, and which have recently been devoted to the tree crops.

REGIONAL SLOPE DISTRIBUTION

In the present case study the average slope map and an enumeration of aerial distribution of the slope between 2° interval of slope groups indicate that there is uneven distribution of slope throughout the entire area. About 93.92 per cent of the total area lies between slope groups of below 2° and 2°-4°. And it occupies 42 per cent of the net area sown in the district. While the highest slope value from 6° to 8° covers only 0.94 per cent (100 sq km) of the total area. The slope at the foothills extends from 4° to 6° and covers only 5.14 per cent, i.e., about 550 sq km of the total area, and has only 2.89 per cent of net sown area.

The landuse mapping units of the study area have been discussed geomorphic regionwise. The landuse legend and the extent of area under different landuse are furnished in Table 8.2. The area was divided into three land systems based on the landsat imageries which show the similarities of landforms, land units surficial deposits and landuse. A few check points were verified in the field during the personal observations, after that a landuse map (Fig. 8.3) was prepared to comprehend the landuse of Sawai Madhopur district.

The following are the three land systems recognised in the district, shown on geomorphological map (Fig. 6.1).

- Structural Hills,
- Dangland Upland, and
- Alluvial Plains.

Structural Hill System

This system consist of hills of the Aravallis and Vindhyan groups. The 300 metres contour line marks the lower boundary of the hilly section right from Bhagawatgarh in the south-west to the Alwar series near Lewali in the north-east. The maximum height is about 527 metres at Lewali. These hills are composed of the older Gwalior rocks and stratified Vindhyan formation in the east and Alwar series in the west along the boundary line with Jaipur. The Great Boundary Fault which runs along the hills, divides the Vindhyans from the Gwaliors.

The drainage of the structural hill region is different in many respects. The subsequent streams which descend from the south-eastern falls of these hills join the Chambal at the right angle. On the whole the drainage pattern is irregular. Most of the rivers of Sawai Madhopur are structurally controlled.

Shallow soils are scattered in almost all foothills of Karauli, Sapotra, Khandar and Sawai Madhopur tahsils. Soils of this zone are of light texture and yellowish brown in colour because of their development on the sandstones and quartzites. On the slates and shales of the Gwalior system, the soils are fine textured but less favourable for the growth of vegetation and crops. The soils on the Gwalior dolerite on the way from Sawai Madhopur to Ranthambhor fort, are black in colour and closely resemble the black cotton soils of the Malwa plateau.

FIG. 8.3

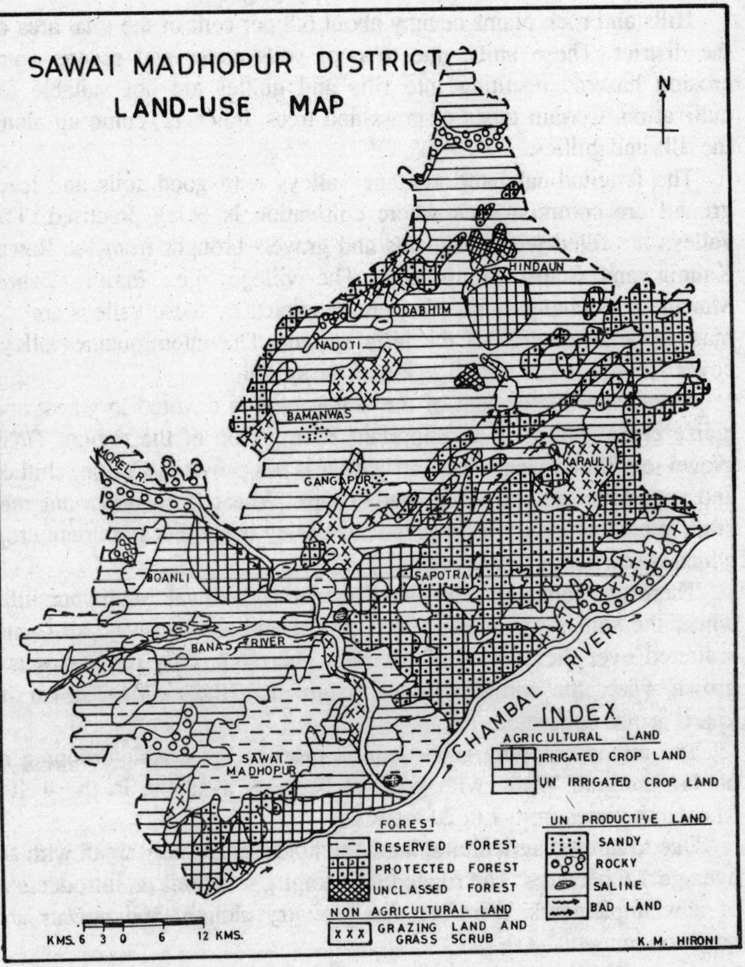

The Delhi and Vindhyan formations are thickly wooded, bulk of such forests are confined to hills in Sawai Madhopur, Khandar, Karauli and Sapotra tahsils. The principal species found here are *Dhok (Anogeissus pendula)*, *Tendu (Deospyros tomentora)*, *Kher (Acacia catechu)*, *Raunj (Acacia leucopholoea)*, *Ber (Zizyphus mauritiana)* etc. In addition, grassy blanks occur on the flat tops and gentle slopes of Sawai Madhopur and Khandar hills. These provide the main grazing grounds for the cattle. The forest areas (reserved, protected and unclassed) are marked on the landuse map (Fig. 8.3).

Hills and rock plains occupy about 6.8 per cent of the total area of the district. These units, due to poor soils cover and severe water erosion hazards resulting into rills and gullies are not suitable for cultivation. Certain types of grass and trees, however, come up along the rills and gullies.

The longitudinal inter-montane valleys with good soils and level ground are common sites where cultivation is being practised. The valleys are filled with sediments and gravels brought from the Rewa, Kaimur and Semri group hills. The villages i.e., Inaitis, Dabra, Makanpur, Mohanpur, Kalederj etc. occupied by these valleys are the main agrarian centres of the hilly system. The intermontane valleys cover 225 sq km out of 650 sq km of the system.

More than 60 per cent of the arable land is devoted to wheat and maize crops. Maize is an important Kharif crop of the region. *Til* is grown to a little extent where irrigation is not possible. Cotton, chillies and sugarcane are the other kharif crops. Wheat is an important rabi crop. Wheat generally follows maize. Barley is another important crop which is sown mixed with wheat.

There are some parts in the Khandar and Sawai Madhopur hills where the soil is too shallow, and gravel and stone pieces are found scattered over the surface of the soil. Therefore, only rabi crops are grown where the soil is light in texture near the *nullahs*. *Jowar* in kharif is also cultivated.

The mixed cropping is a common practice but double-cropping is almost unusual. Water with good recharge is available in the wells. The depth varies from 7 to 20 metres.

Due to limited agricultural land, the holdings are very small with an average 1.6 hectares. The rugged topography sets limit on introduction of new implements, therefore, *hal* (country plough) and *bakhar* are common in use.

The Dangland Upland System

This upland agricultural region runs from the north-east of the Banas water gap up to the boundary with Dholpur. The Upper Bhandar sandstone forms the western boundary while the Sirbu shales and the Bhandar limestone are extend on the eastern side along the Chambal river. It slopes the north-east and the south-east. The height varies from 300 metres to 450 metres.

principal crops in kharif are *bajra, jowar,* pulses and groundnut which are cultivated under rainfed condition and secondary crops are wheat, barley, sugarcane grown under irrigated conditions. The unirrigated lands occurring on the vast stretches, are cultivated with *bajra* or *jowar* in kharif season and mustard and wheat mixed crops in the rabi season. Old deposits occur between the hills and sub-recent deposits in the fluvial plains. *Bajra, jowar* and pulses are grown during Kharif whereas, wheat, barley during rabi season.

The badland or ravine belt is extended from the Banas water gap to the north-east up to district boundary known as the badland region. Almost all the streams of the district forms the ravine topography. The depth and elevations of ravine areas differ from place to place. The depth varies from 20 to 30 metres. It depends on the soil characteristics, nature of slope and intensity of vertical corrosion by the ephemeral streams. The side and head scarp are devoid of vegetation. The alluvial knolls are common in the midst of ravines, which look like Mesa topography.

The area is highly dissected by water erosion, having deep soils with texture varying from sandy loam to loam. *Kankar* layer is found at 1 to 2 metres below the surface. Most of the fertile land has gone out of the plough due to fluvial erosion.

Slip off slopes, ravine bottoms and the marginal sloping areas are the main cultivable areas where agriculture is being practised. The ravine infested tahsils Karauli, Sapotra and Khandar are having very little net sown area i.e. 22.1 per cent, 20.7 per cent and 34.0 per cent respectively. The main crop of kharif is *bajra* and barley is grown in the rabi season. Pulses including *moong, arhar, jowar* and gram are other important crops in this unit.

TABLE 8.3: Suggested Landuse based on Land System, Land Units, Landuse Capability and Limitations

Land System

Structural Hills

Land Units

Rocky, Aravalli narrow flat topped hills, moderate inclination (4°-6°); sharp, broad, folded, faulted, Delhi and Vindhyan Super Group, height above 300 metres, inter-montane colluvial plain with debris and foot hill slope (2°-4°), elevation range 210 metres- 280 metres.

Description/Physical Characteristics

Strike ridges, gneiss in broken chain, quartzites, conglomerate and schists; longitudinal valleys, eroded anticlines, dolerite, shales, hamatite shales; highly rugged and undulating 300-527 metres, soils shallow, texture loam and sandy loam, gravels, stone oftenly found, gravel and sand (colluvium) on debris slopes; gravel, and *Kankar* in foot slopes and in valleys. Few plots of wastelands due to gullying.

Drainage

Adequate drainage; with moderate permeability, poor on steep slopes.

Erosion

Soil erosion and gullying, severe water erosion problems.

Capability and Limitations

Severe limitations, suited for forests; raising pastures; not suited for cultivation, anogeissus pendule forests, Raunj (Acacia leucopuloea), Tendu (Diospyros melanoxylon), Salar (Boswelliaserratial) on upper slopes; herbs and grasses on lower slopes and on isolated hills / hillocks.

Present Landuse

Forest and scrub bare hill slopes, degraded forest, grazing, quarring of rock, mostly barren rocky inferior species as Darshan, Tor, invaded forest, Maize — important Kharif crops. Wheat — Chief rabi crop. Mixed cropping is common.

Potential/Recommended Landuse

Felling of trees to be checked to avoid soil erosion and gullying, quarring of rock, over grazing, and inferior species to be stopped, suitable for tree plantations, developing pastures and dairy, very little possibility of agricultural development due to rugged topography.

Land System

Dangland plateau

Land Units

Gentle to broad uplands; low to broad low lands; gentle rounded mesas, deep cut gorges of streams, Slope (2°-4°); highly faulty, foot hills of moderate inclination (4°-6°); Valley fills, nearly level to gently sloping valley (1°-3°).

Description/Physical Characteristics

Upper Bhander sandstone dominates, Sirbu shales and Bhandar limestones, dissected and undulating, elevation 300-450 metres, slope N.E. and S.E. soils moderately deep thin at places, sandy, loam to loamy texture, yellowish brown; little salinity in lowlands, pH: 7.2 to 9.0, poor in humus, nitrogen, electrical conductivity 0.30 to 1.5 m mhos/cm.

Drainage

Moderate on upland, good on low lands.

Erosion

Silting of tanks due to occasional erosion of intensively cultivated uplands.

Capability and Limitations

Moderate limitations, low watertable show availability of regular water tanks and wells in low lands, moderate permeability, wasteland for pasture and forest, a Vindhyan aquifers, moderate discharge, water table 4 to 15 metres.

Present Landuse

Drycrops; *bajra, jowar,* wheat; sugarcane at some places; groundnut and pulses, gram; masur, wet crops (paddy) in valley fills.

Potential/Recommended Landuse

Sugarcane, cotton (deep rooted crops) should not be taken on shallow soils. Upper slopes suitable for pastures. Salt tolerant crop i.e. barley and wheat should be taken up. Flooding of saline soil, dry and wet crops (provided water is available in valley fills). This agricultural region may be specialised for forests and grasses or fodder crops.

Land System

Alluvial plain

Land Units

Unconsolidated alluvium deposits, flood plains, ancient channels and levees, slope 1° to 2°, river beds 1° or less than 30'; ravine belt (1°-3°), flats riverine plain, elevation 240-280 metres.

Description/Physical Characteristics

Recent to sub-recent deposits, alluvial underlain sandstones at some places; soils deep to heavy deep, light olive brown to dark olive, light to medium texture, dissected by ravines and gullies, salinity at few places, sandy loam to loam, pH: 7.8 to 8.4 and electrical conductivity 0.3 to 1.0 m to 1.0 m Mhos /cm.

Drainage

Adequate and good surface drainage.

Erosion

Severe water erosion problem, bank erosion during floods.

Capability and Limitations

Good irrigable land, adequate drainage is limitation, high water table (at 4 metres depth in ancient channels), 5 to 14 metres in fluvial plain, flood hazards common.

Present Landuse

Wheat, paddy, maize, gram on irrigated land, *bajra, jowar,* groundnut on unirrigated land, sugarcane at some places. Scrub on ravine.

Potential/Recommended Landuse

Can almost grow all crops in the above mentioned section of 1 and 2. Sugarcane, cotton, gram and pulses, til should be taken up on large scale where irrigation is available, forests on ravine land.

9

SUMMARY AND LANDUSE PLANNING

SUMMARY

THE INTERPLAY between physical elements and human factors are extremely complex and multidimensional, in the relationship that exist between man and land, is of paramount importance. In a densely populated country like India and a underdeveloped State like Rajasthan, feeding the growing population, on a traditional agricultural system, becomes a difficult task. It is in this context correct measurement and evaluation of land resource base becomes absolutely necessary to bring the processes of agricultural landuse and crop production on a sound genetic footing. This has great relevance for an agricultural area such as present study area where cultivation has been carried out since times immemorial and in which a high proportion of rural population is dependent on primary vocation. The objectives of sustained production can only be achieved through an analysis of morphological character of the region. As geomorphological analysis or approach attempts to express the integration of all elements of the land complex, recognised the casual links between them through an understanding of the genesis of landform themselves.

The preceeding chapters of the present study, give a systematic account of geomorphological character of the region, existing landuse and a decadal change in landuse pattern. The study reveals that the impact of geomorphology is multifaceted, as various landforms and configuration of land surface determine land utilisation types and changes that have occurred as result of change in morphological character.

In Sawai Madhopur district, agriculture and animal husbandry are predominant sources of occupation. Because of the topographical constrains, the scope of irrigation is very limited and therefore, the cultivation depends mostly on monsoonal rainfall. Physical conditions like landforms, soils and distribution of water resources pose a serious constraints to cropping pattern and practices. The foregoing discussion throughout the study presents a synthesised account of geomorphology and landuse. The main findings of the study are being summarised in the following pages:

1. As has been discussed earlier the study area has a unique location between the south-eastern extension of the Aravallis and north-western fringe of the Vindhyan Basin. The geomorphic history is therefore closely linked with the evolution of these systems. The landforms or morphology has evolved through various endogenetic and exogenetic forces. Various sets of landforms have been developed according to the nature of rocks of Aravallis system and the Vindhyan system. Faults and lineaments have controlled the evolution of various forms of topography in the area.
2. Climate of the district is semi-arid. The region experiences scanty to moderate rainfall. It is characterised by torrential nature. Rainfall is mainly concentrated in monsoon period. Temperatures are generally high during May and June and minimum in December and January. Both daily and annual range of temperatures are high. The rainfall pattern and range of temperature pose limits on agricultural practices of the district.
3. The soils of the region are resulted from various factors like climate, relief, rock types and vegetation. On the basis of their morphological and textural characteristics, the soils of the district have been classified into four types i.e. deep and medium black and greyish, deep light textured and yellow-brown, shallow foothills light brown soils and deep light, ravined light brown soils.
4. The study of fluvial morphology of the district reveals that the underlying geological structures controls the evolution of drainage lines. The diversion of the Banas and alignment of the Chambal parallel to the Great Boundary Fault is profoundly controlled by the Cretaceous tectonic movements. The study of river courses and the analysis of their long profiles reveal that the topography is in mature stage but the streams have a tendency of rejuvenation as a consequences of neotectonic activity.

The stream frequency ranges between 0 to 1.4 per sq unit (25 kilometres). The category of low frequency (0.50) covers about 79.9 per cent of the total area, mostly lying on alluvial plains. The drainage density also shows a similarity with the stream frequency. It ranges between 0 to 1.23 per sq unit.

5. The analysis of flood morphology of Sawai Madhopur district gives an over all picture of the river regimes. Unprecedented and prolonged rainfall during few days of monsoonal period is the most common cause of flooding. Besides this, topography, geology, palaeo-drainage, vegetation, source areas and landuse practices have their own impact on frequency of floods. The following are the resultant problems of flooding in the area under study: high rainfall with maximum intensity results into heavy downpour which decelerate the infiltration of water and increase runoff which takes the course of maximum overland flow and through it contributes the maximum value of water to the Banas, the Morel and the Gambhir rivers and through its several tributaries and *nullahs*.

   The lack of tree cover along the rivers also increases runoff and overland flow. The relationship between runoff, sediment yields, rainfall and discharge are directly related with each other.

   The condition at the confluence of the Banas and Morel, is very precarious. Both the rivers with several tributaries accumulate the water near Namada and Haroti which are the most flood prone areas, create high magnitude flood peaks. This water spreads over Bamanwas, Boanli and Gangapur tahsils. While the Gambhir river taking water from the Dangland through Panchai, Manchi river and makes confluence with river Churhao and plays havoc in Todabhim and Hindaun tahsils.

   Valley side slopes are ploughed down to the channel in transverse furrows, during 'rabi season' (winter season) and the farms are seldom irrigated. After the crops are harvested in the summer season these ploughed fields with the first summer showers, the dried soils soaked with water, are slumped into the river bed by over-flowed flow. This slumping of the moistened soils results in the gradual silting of the river bed. On the other hand, the cultivation of valley side slopes reduces the gradient of the bank. These two processes flatten the valley and thus reduce the holding capacity of the water. With the result the river take, (Gambhir and Banas), very little time in attaining their full bank capacity and afterwards water spreads over the valley side.

Besides this, shifting of the course of the Morel river and ruthless exploitation of vegetation are also responsible for the flood hazards in the district.

6. The study also reveals that ravine and gully erosion is also a very serious problem of agriculture which has resulted by neotectonic activity and promoted by faulty landuse practices. The more serious ravine erosion problem occurs along the Banas-Morel, the Banas-Chambal, the Gambhir and over the Dangland slopes and longitudinal weaker zone's valleys. It is found that ravines are one of the features developing due to rejuvenation and motivated due to defective landuse practices.
7. On the basis of various landforms components the district has been divided into three major geomorphic regions and five sub-regions. The analysis of these regions, gives an insight into potentials and provide a sound base for rational landuse, soil and water conservation, development and management of the district.
8. In the present study an attempt has also been made to study and analyse the existing land utilisation. The 300 metres contour running north to south divides the district broadly into two parts. The eastern portion is mainly non-arable while the western is arable.
9. The non-arable includes forests, land put to non-agricultural use, barren and uncultivable and covers 38.31 per cent (4,04,148 hectares) of the total area of the district. Only 1.01 per cent non-arable land has decreased in the past decade (1976-86). This change poses a serious threat to the cultivated land while the population of the district has increased 29.4 per cent in the same period.
10. The percentage of forests in the district is 22.47. Experts in soil management usually recommends that a minimum of 30 to 33 per cent of the total land be forested. If we take this standard, almost all the tahsils of the district have very low standards except Karauli (40.60%), Sapotra (52.1%) and Khandar (34.79%). The lowest forest cover is in the Hindaun (2.34%), Mahwa (2.6%) and Boanli (3.57%). In the last decade only Karauli (4%), Sapotra (16.8%), and Khandar (5.7%) have

shown an increase in the forests area. Thus the remaining tahsils need much attention for evolving a strategy for development and protection of forest cover.

11. The study area has not shown a marked increase in net area sown. In 1975-76 the net area sown was 45.25 per cent and it was 46.00 per cent in 1985-86. There was a slight increase of 0.75 per cent. But there is still a lot of scope for accelerating this rate of growth. However, it may be noted that there is little scope for increasing the area under cultivation except through the reclamation or saline, alkaline and other wastelands. Even the fallow land has slightly increased (0.25%) instead of showing a decline in the decade.
12. A regional synthesis of landuse is a primary need. The district witnesses pockets of agricultural land. For optimum utilisation of such pockets, the study of slope is a must. Intermontane valleys have fair scope for agricultural development with assured water supply. Over the Dangland the Vindhyan uplands have mixed agriculture with poor fallow and scrub-pasture. Panchna canal irrigation has facilitated cultivation and double-cropping. Areas not receiving sufficient rain or irrigation and have a little scope for irrigation are left fallow. The valley fills are fertile depression and the intermontane valleys have enough potentiality for increasing arable land and intensive farming.
13. The alluvial plains present a unique picture of intensive agricultural area having more than 70 per cent area sown (Mahwa 75.00%; Todabhim 70.37%). Similarly, agriculture predominates in Nadoti (66.15%), Gangapur (64.61%), and Bamanwas (63.5%). But Karauli (22.1%), Sapotra (20.71%) and Khandar (34.0%) have a very low percentage of net area sown due to hilly tract and lack of irrigation facilities and lack of knowledge of upland agriculture practices. Still there is scope to bringing more land under the cultivation in Mahwa, Hindaun and Todabhim, since the adjoining tahsils of Bharatpur are owing above 90 per cent net area sown. Nadoti, Gangapur and Bamanwas have also potentiality of increase the area. The sandy undulating alluvial plains are suitable for growing grasses for few years and after the stabilisation sand and improvement in their agricultural productivity these plains could be put under cultivation.

LANDUSE PLANNING

For better landuse planning of the district, the following recommendations may be made.

1. In a decade (1975-76 to 1985-86) only 0.75 per cent of the net area sown has increased. This slow increase can be revamped through increase in irrigation. There is a fairly good scope for increasing the area under irrigation as the well normally have good recharge and water is also good in the Boanli, Bamanwas, Gangapur and along the Chambal river, in the valley fills. Rocky/gravally foothills should be capitalised for water harvesting runoff collection and pasture establishment.

   Colluvial plains (intermontane) extending in a narrow tract, from Nimoda to Wazirpur, having potential for agriculture, because of the favourable physical conditions and high water-table from 5 to 18 metres.
2. The district in 1985-86, had 24.9 per cent of the cropped area (5,10,000 hectares) which was provided with irrigation facilities from different sources. There is about 70 per cent of the total cropped area which is still unirrigated. Thus, it becomes essential to extend irrigation facilities from existing tanks, canals, and new digging of wells and canal construction. The new irrigation facilities can very easily convert 49,000 hectares of fallow land into cultivated land out of which the Dangland alone will account for 29,000 hectares.
3. On the structural hills there is very little possibility of agricultural development due to rugged topography. It is advisable to grow only tree plantation and pastures for dairy industry. Falling of trees to be checked to avoid soil erosion and gullying. Besides this over-grazing be stopped.
4. Dangland plateau and the foothills of the areas should be capitalised for water harvesting runoff collection and pastures establishment. Where soils are shallow the deep rooted crops like sugarcane and cotton should not be allowed. In the saline older alluvial plain near the foot hills, the salt-tolerant crops i.e. wheat and barley should be grown. These foothill plains should not be cultivated every year, otherwise the salinity problem will increase. The valleyfills are the suitable grounds for future agriculture extension.

5. The alluvial plain can almost grow all crops like sugarcane, cotton, groundnut, gram, pulses and *til* etc., which has good facilities of irrigation. In the areas (Boanli), where salinity due to the irrigation has cropped up, the irrigation with sprinkler and drip has been suggested with some changes of cropping pattern. There is a good scope for increasing the area under irrigation as the wells normally have good recharge and water also is good in Gangapur, Nadoti, Todabhim, Boanli and Mahawa tahsils.
6. In the district a detailed knowledge of geomorphological conditions for understanding the process of the formation and degradation of soils and landscapes, is needed. Dynamism of the slope development should be taken into account while planning the cultivation of undulating terrain. In the district gently sloping area with a slope value of 3° and a moderate slope of 6° are suggested to show suitability for cropping. With increasing slope angle, there is an increase in the slope instability and hence it is essential to understand the relationship between slope and landuse category. The study of geo-hydrology is an essential requisite for sound, landuse planning. In the area the main source of ground water is alluvium of Quaternary age. The depth of water level is 3 to 12 metres in Boanli, Bamanwas, Todabhim, Nadoti and Mahuwa. There is a great scope of improvement of well irrigation. Valleyfills along the Chambal river have aquifer of good discharge. Fracture zones of sandstone and limestone of the Vindhyan system can also be utilised for well digging. Identification of palaeo-channels in the area, will help to arrest the flood hazards.
7. The deep, light-yellow brown soil along the Chambal river is exposed to water erosion. Due to the moderate slopes, uneven and undulating topography and the lack of soil and water conservation measures, very little rainfall enters the soils and used by the crop plants. Most of the water is lost through surface water. It is essential to bund the fields and level the hummocks in order to check erosion. In the west of the Dangland shallow, light brown soils, specially in Hindaun, Karauli, Sapotra and Sawai Madhopur, are suitable for developing only pastures and forests.
8. Salinity, specially in Sawai Madhopur, Sapotra, Nadoti and Boanli tahsils is the main problem. Green manuring like

Dhaincha should be introduced every third year to reclaim the saline soil. In addition to this salt tolerant crops like barley and wheat should be introduced. Where the water of good quality is freely available flooding of saline soils may be practised to remove surface salt. For the areas affected by the sodic problem (Boanli, Sawai Madhopur and Hindaun blocks), addition of gypsum together with high does of farm yard manure or compost is recommended. Powdered gypsum at the rate of 5 to 6 tonnes/hectare should be introduced before the on set of monsoon.

For the irrigated crops, nitrogenous fertilizers may be added in split doses – phosphorus and potash – may be sprinkled at the time of the sowing of the crops.

9. The district witnesses floods whenever there are heavy rains. Bamanwas, Boanli, Todabhim and Gangapur tahsils are the worst affected areas. Statistics show that the phenomenon of floods occurs every second year. In 1981 out of 59,000 hectares of the arable land about 4,000 hectares land was rendered useless.

   Large scale planning is required in order to minimise the loss and damages caused by floods. To begin with, a geographical survey of the area must be undertaken.

10. The condition at the confluence of the Banas with Morel (near Haroti and Namada) is more serious as the rivers have straightened their courses by leaving their present confluence during 1981 flood. Now the river Banas meets the Morel about 10-15 kilometres northward upstream. But during rainy season the palaeo-channel again revive their courses which results into the erosion of hundreds of hectares of cultivable land in Bhadoti, Biloli, Chor Malarna, Bhukha and Gauhwapur (Boanli), Jirofa, Aroda and Haroti (Sapotra) villages. Flood diversion through construction of bypass channels on the Banas and the Morel are recommended, to curtail the intensity of flood water at the confluence.

    The flooding is not a simple case of a river toppling its banks. What is needed in this case is a careful study and demarcation of all the disorganised courses before planning any flood control measures. There is also the need to keep in mind this fact when structures like dams are planned for such areas.

11. Instead of cultivating the valley sides, the farmers should be persuaded to grow eucalyptus groves which in addition check the erosion of valley sides and the slumping of soils into river bed. This will provide more economic wealth to the farmers than the income from crops.
12. Ravines are spreading over a large area of the district. Scientific criteria are needed to study the physical characteristics, soils and locational factors, quantitative data about various types of ravines (G_1, G_2 and G_3) etc. Based on these criteria, the ravine areas could be developed for the benefit of the community.

    Soil survey should be carried out with the help of aerial photographs, taking a village map as the base, the whole ravine system along a particular river or tributary be selected as a unit with self contained water sheds for general planning like the Banas-Morel, the Gambhir and the Chambal should be taken up. Ravine areas be classified as suggested below.

Ravine Reclamability Classification for Agricultural

Class I: Fit for reclamation into agricultural land with minor reclamation operations. These lands are generally of G_1. To some extent G_2 type of ravines.

Class II: Fit for reclamation into agricultural land with medium intensity, reclamation operations (G_2).

Class III: Fit for reclamation into agricultural land with major reclamation measures. Deep ravines classified as G_3.

Class IV: Fit for horticulture with reclamation operations for small width horticulture terraces (mostly G_3).

Ravine Reclamability Classification for Non-agricultural

Class V: Fit for grassland and forestry by closure alone.

Class VI: Fit for grassland and forestry by closure and intensive afforestation measures.

Class VII: Not fir for even regular grassland and forestry but fit for utilisation as a waterway ravine, water-storage or other such purposes.

Generally the shallow ravines may be brought under cultivation. Ravine with large watershed areas will require diversion of runoff and construction of ravine head control structures.

After marking reclamation classes, the following uses may be suggested for ravine lands:

(i) Crop management practices like use of legumes or grass crops in rotation at least once in five years, for instance, often give a high degree of protection from sheet erosion.

(ii) Permanent vegetation should be drawn on the marginal lands or ravines according to the hydrological conditions. Afforestation belt should be along rivers. Wild life reserve may also be planned where it is needed.

(iii) On the reclaimed lands green manuring and chemical fertilizers should be used for about 3-5 years for restoring soil fertility. After this application such crops as groundnut and gram should be grown which have greater soil binding capacity. Similar studies at Kota (ICAR) in Chambal ravinous area – the three legumes studies (Cowpea, moong and groundnut). Cowpea gave minimum runoff and soil loss followed by *moong* and groundnut. Under various cropping patterns, grasses like *Dichanthium* annulatum were recorded as the most efficient in conserving soil and moisture.

(iv) Erection of earthen or masonry dams or bush dams, breaking and levelling up of the ravines, creation of diversion channels which would divert the water of the gullies. Filling up the depression formed along roads and railways, field bending and embodiments, etc. are the conservation methods.

(v) Boanli, Gangapur, Bamanwas and Sawai Madhopur tahsils are more prone to sheet erosion. The measures like contour-ploughing, strip cultivation, terracing, horticulture or bamboo cultivation should be practised.

(vi) A detailed irrigation plan should be prepared in the area like Panchna dam.

13. Regarding the planned land utilisation in the district, the forest has not been considered as an economic sector like agriculture. Certain suggestions which, if implemented, most likely will revamp the forest economy of the district.

Sawai Madhopur (19.69%), Hindaun (2.34%) and Gangapur (3.26%) tahsils need special attention of afforestation. In Sawai

Madhopur tahsil – anogeissus pendula forests and good species of Polda (*Apluda mutica*), Lampla (*Aristida*), Kali lamp (*Hetropocon controtus*) and *Dhok* etc., trees are toppled due to overgrazing, excessive felling of the trees and shrubs for fodder, fuel and other purposes. It may be suggested that the degraded forests be replanted and the area under barren and uncultivable heads (6.50%) be developed into reserved forests.

In Gangapur, Todabhim, Nadoti where water erosion is dominating problem and percentage of land under forest is very low. Soils are loam to clay loam, salinity is increasing. Therefore, on sandy soils, the species should possess thick foliage on stem to combat the drifting sand. The consecutive rows of Poplers (*Terminalia arjuna, Pongamia pinate*) should be planted. In case of loamy soils, water logging and the presence of *Kankers* nodules, the promising species for planting are *Prosopis juliflora, Accacia nilotica, Dalbergin sissoo, Pongamia pinnata* etc. During the field observation weeding was found on *usar* soils, which is harmful. It should not be allowed.

Though Khandar, Sapotra and Karauli tahsils have shown tremendous increase in forests area during the decade (1975-76 to 1985-86), but Teli-Ki-Panseri hills (Karauli). Ranwatzora Dungar, Ranthambhor hills (Sawai Madhopur) and Boanli hills etc., all tell a sad tale of destruction of vegetation. Most of the top soil has been washed away. Trees are difficult to plant on these skeletal soils. These areas should first be planted with shrubs. Foot hills of Hindaun tahsil are suitable for developing pastures.

Ravines occupy vast tracts of the district. Planting should be carried out in two stages. In the first stage emphasis should be on gully plugging. After the area has been under protection for sometime and movement of soil has been partly controlled through gully plugs, trees, bamboos and grasses should be planted at a suitable places.

APPENDICES

APPENDIX I

Monthly Temperature, Relative Humidity, Mean Wind Speed, Thunder, Dust-storm and Evaporation Condition (1925-1980) at Sawai Madhopur

Sl. No.	Item	MONTHS											
		Jan	Feb	March	April	May	June	July	Aug	Sept	Oct	Nov	Dec
1.	Lowest Temperature in the month °C	1.8	3.9	8.9	14.0	20.3	23.2	23.3	23.3	20.9	11.1	3.9	3.3
2.	Daily Minimum Temperature °C	8.1	9.8	15.9	21.5	27.5	30.5	27.0	25.8	24.3	19.2	11.2	8.4
3.	Mean Monthly Temperature °C	15.5	18.8	24.0	30.1	35.0	36.1	30.6	29.3	28.9	26.1	20.1	16.7
4.	Daily Minimum Temperature °C	22.9	27.0	32.1	38.7	42.4	41.8	34.1	32.8	33.6	32.9	29.1	25.1
5.	Highest Temperature in the month °C	30.2	34.7	39.1	43.8	46.7	47.1	42.2	39.0	37.4	38.2	35.0	31.3
6.	Relative Humidity in Percentage	77	62	60	40	33	46	79	85	81	72	61	70

Contd.

APPENDIX I *Contd.*

Temperature and Humidity Chart for Kota and Tonk

	Jan	Feb	March	April	May	June	July	Aug	Sept	Oct	Nov	Dec
KOTA:												
1. Temperature in °C	18.3	21.25	21.3	26.3	35.25	34.4	31.4	29.45	29.3	26.8	22.5	19.25
2. Humidity in per cent	64	51	51	24	28	47	74	81	73	53	51	61
TONK:												
1. Temperature in °C	14.1	18.75	24.55	30.05	34.05	34.15	31.0	28.7	28.15	20.25	19.75	15.50
2. Humidity in per cent	56.5	48.05	37.55	39.5	34.85	51.55	71.8	81.83	74.0	63.5	63.5	64.95

Source: Meteorological Department, Western Circle, Jaipur.

APPENDIX II

Rainfall Record From 1891-1986: Sawai Madhopur

Year				*Year*				*Year*			
1891	29.6	-6.2	-17.8	1923	48.0	+11.2	+37.4	1955	39.3	+4.5	+12.9
1892	45.6	+10.8	+31.0	1924	40.6	+8.8	+16.6	1956	59.1	+24.3	+69.8
1893	31.1	-3.7	-10.6	1925	23.3	-11.5	-33.0	1957	54.3	+19.5	+66.0
1894	46.3	+11.5	+33.0	1926	31.1	-3.7	-10.6	1958	39.6	+4.8	+13.8
1895	24.5	-10.3	-29.6	1927	22.9	—	-5.4	1959	51.3	+16.5	+47.3
1896	23.5	-11.3	-32.5	1928	25.1	-8.7	-27.8	1960	27.4	-7.5	21.5
1897	29.8	-5.0	-14.4	1929	22.3	-12.5	-35.9	1961	21.6	-13.2	-37.4
1898	22.1	-12.7	-36.5	1930	38.4	+3.6	+10.3	1962	26.1	-8.7	-25.0
1899	23.5	-11.3	-32.5	1931	41.5	+6.7	+19.3	1963	29.4	-5.4	-15.5
1900	40.7	+5.9	+17.9	1932	34.5	-0.3	+0.8	1964	37.5	+27.0	+7.7
1901	17.1	-17.7	-50.9	1933	67.6	+32.8	+94.3	1965	12.7	-22.1	-63.5
1902	28.1	-6.7	-16.4	1934	59.2	+24.4	+70.1	1971	89.5		
1903	25.4	-9.4	-27.0	1935	48.1	+13.3	+38.2	1972	94.1		
1904	45.0	+9.8	+28.1	1936	41.2	+6.4	+18.3	1973	82.9		
1905	7.9	-26.9	-74.4	1937	42.2	+7.4	+21.3	1974	90.5		
1906	19.8	-15.0	-43.1	1938	19.1	-51.7	-45.1	1975	111.3		
1907	28.5	-6.3	-18.1	1939	11.9	-22.9	-65.8	1976	81.0		
1908	37.7	+2.9	+8.3	1940	22.3	-12.5	-35.9	1977	93.3		
1909	25.5	-9.3	-26.7	1945	70.1	+35.3	+101.5	1978	84.6		
1910	27.7	-7.1	-20.1	1946	54.2	+19.5	+56.0	1979	59.2		
1911	22.8	-12.0	35.5	1947	27.3	-7.5	-21.5	1980	64.0		
1912	34.0	-0.8	-2.3	1948	—	—	—	1981	66.4		
1913	10.8	-24.0	69.0	1949	29.9	-4.9	-14.0	1982	86.28		
1918	9.3	-25.5	-73.3	1950	39.7	+4.9	+14.0	1983	99.2		
1919	52.8	+18.0	+51.9	1951	14.3	-20.5	-60.4	1984	47.8		
1920	26.0	-8.8	-25.3	1952	32.7	-2.1	-6.0	1985	72.3		
1921	29.6	-5.2	-14.9	1953	22.8	-12.0	-34.5	1986	71.2		
1922	27.9	-6.9	-19.8	1954	3.4	-1.4	-4.0				

APPENDIX III

Normal Monthly Rainfall in Sawai Madhopur District

Place	Jan	Feb	Mar	April	May	June	July	Aug	Sept	Oct	Nov	Dec
Sawai Madhopur	8	5	6	2	6	78	336	306	124	21	2	6
Khandar	7	3	8	5	6	86	227	231	129	11	1	5
Boanli	7											
Gangapur	9	6	5	4	7	52	227	223	101	15	3	5
Hindaun	10	6	7	4	7	49	219	227	107	14	4	5
Todabhim	11	6	6	3	8	66	188	149	100	16	3	7
Mahuwa	10	10	6	4	10	41	180	180	105	18	2	8
Karauli	11	8	5	4	10	53	241	244	108	16	4	5
Sapotra	10	—	—	—	—	—	—	—	—	—	—	—
Bamanwas	9											
Nadoti	10											

Source: Hydrology Department, Jaipur

APPENDIX IV

Seasonal Rainfall Intensity in Sawai Madhopur District

Place	Pre-Monsoon	Monsoon	Post Monsoon	Winter period or season
Sawai Madhopur	3.130	24.215	6.119	3.125
Khandar	3.460	18.940	6.347	3.104
Gangapur	4.427	24.553	3.282	4.968
Hindaun	3.979	18.101	3.336	5.725
Todabhim	3.286	20.024	3.938	2.541
Mahuwa	2.963	16.619	6.104	6.645
Karauli	3.402	19.993	7.699	6.382
Boanli	7.833	22.058	5.241	1.333
Sapotra	3.810	20.876	4.733	5.791
Bamanwas	5.202	24.423	3.306	4.170
Nadoti	2.791	19.396	3.842	3.312

Source: Hydrology Department, Jaipur

APPENDIX VIII

Land Utilisation Area Classification (hectares) 1975-76

Sl. No.	Name of the Tahsil/ District	Total Geographical area		Forest	Not available for cultivation			Other un-cultivated (excluding) fallow land				Fallow land			Net area sown	Total cropped area	Area sown more than once
		According to village survey	According to village papers		Land put non-agricultural uses	Barron and uncultivable lands	Total	Permanent pasture and grazing lands	Land under misc. trees	Culturable waste	Total	Other fallow land	Current fallow land	Total			
1	2	3	4	5	6	7	8	9	10	11	12	13	14	15	16	17	18
1.	Sawai Madhopur	164466	164466	34347	10240	4802	23804	8556	85	6698	15339	3809	5445	9254	81722	84658	2936
2.	Khandar	96014	96014	26897	905	8032	16248	11188	11	7074	18273	1594	2476	4070	30526	30935	459
3.	Boanli	101584	101584	2534	3068	1852	16543	7010	12	5512	12535	4322	6790	11112	58860	63479	4619
4.	Gangapur	64447	64447	2053	1702	1256	5892	4485	17	4256	8758	1622	4679	6243	41451	48862	7411
5.	Bamanwas	73925	73925	3518	2440	5245	9862	5069	12	3944	9025	1754	3514	5268	46252	53447	7195
6.	Nadoti	65285	65285	8611	3300	2414	7342	1791	29	2829	4643	1884	3049	4633	40050	46173	6123
7.	Hindaun	64095	64095	1470	1106	3046	10797	7195	51	2293	9539	743	1983	2726	39563	57665	18102
8.	Todabhim	54504	54504	1765	300	3446	6697	3122	56	2722	5900	887	2280	3167	36975	50734	13809
9.	Mahuwa	47801	47801	970	2916	1275	5392	1553	31	1492	3076	596	2177	2773	35590	48840	12250
10.	Karauli	181910	181910	66942	3682	26469	43966	14276	26	9031	23333	3663	4809	8472	39197	50255	11050
11.	Sapotra	140365	140365	49275	3429	34804	46696	6643	43	5491	12177	1747	3456	5203	25014	28300	3286
12.	TOTAL	1054396	1054396	198382	33286	92762	193239	70889	363	51342	122604	22321	40650	62971	477200	569150	91950

Source: Table of Agricultural Statistics of Sawai Madhopur District, 1975-76.

APPENDIX IX

Land Utilisation Area Classification (hectares) 1975-76

Sl. No.	Name of the Tahsil/ District	Total Geographical area		Forest	Not available for cultivation			Other un-cultivated (excluding) fallow land				Fallow land			Net area sown	Total cropped area	Area sown more than once
		According to village survey	According to village papers		Land put non-agricultural	Barron and un-cultivable lands	Total	Permanent pasture and grazing lands	Land under misc. trees	Culturable waste	Total	Other fallow land	Current fallow land	Total			
1	2	3	4	5	6	7	8	9	10	11	12	13	14	15	16	17	18
1.	Sawai Madhopur	164466	164466	32389	5077	23224	28301	6203	65	4418	10686	3040	10115	13755	79935	83534	3619
2.	Khandar	96014	96014	33395	3966	9363	13329	11410	11	1895	13316	1144	2179	3323	32651	33573	922
3.	Boanli	101594	101594	3630	7463	10084	17547	6454	34	3070	9558	4607	9132	13739	57110	63702	6592
4.	Gangapur	64447	64447	2061	1960	5768	7728	3797	25	2408	6230	2166	3831	5997	42431	50172	7741
5.	Bamanwas	73925	73925	3900	1674	8896	10570	4873	9	2381	7263	1564	3835	5399	46793	50268	3475
6.	Nadoti	65285	65285	9213	3728	2969	6697	1883	30	1529	3442	1065	1710	2775	43158	47331	4173
7.	Hindaun	64095	64095	1493	3431	6845	10276	7437	44	1473	8954	1274	1997	3271	40101	58101	18068
8.	Todabhim	54504	54504	2819	3325	3237	6562	2869	93	1315	4282	1051	1749	2800	38041	50277	2236
9.	Mahuwa	47801	47801	1255	3086	2348	5434	1571	39	983	2593	797	1864	2661	35858	47005	11147
10.	Karauli	181910	181910	73868	4929	32273	37202	14549	51	8103	22703	4136	3682	7818	40319	52141	11822
11.	Sapotra	140365	140365	73002	4419	19058	23477	7949	32	2465	10446	2001	2715	4716	28724	36135	7411
	TOTAL	1054396	1054396	237025	43058	124065	167123	68995	438	30040	99473	22845	42809	65654	485121	572337	87206

Source: Tables of Agricultural Statistics of Sawai Madhopur District, 1985-86.

APPENDIX X

Land Utilisation Area Classification (Percentage in Geographical Area 1975-76

Sl. No.	Name of the Tahsil	Forest	Not available for cultivation	Other un-cultivated land excluding fallow land	Fallow land	Net area sown	Total cropped area	Area sown more than once
1.	Sawai Madhopur	20.85	14.46	9.33	5.65	49.6	51.46	1.78
2.	Khandar	28.12	16.97	19.06	4.27	31.79	32.29	0.47
3.	Boanli	2.55	16.2	12.3	10.92	57.94	62.49	4.5
4.	Gangapur	3.25	9.14	13.6	9.76	64.26	75.75	11.48
5.	Bamanwas	4.72	13.5	12.16	7.16	62.5	72.29	9.73
6.	Nadoti	13.16	11.34	7.19	7.09	61.33	70.75	9.37
7.	Hindaun	2.34	16.8	14.8	4.36	61.71	90.79	28.24
8.	Todabhim	3.30	12.40	11.00	5.87	67.8	93.42	25.33
9.	Mahuwa	2.09	11.29	6.48	5.83	74.47	100.8	25.62
10.	Karauli	36.8	24.17	12.82	4.67	21.55	26.10	6.07
11.	Sapotra	35.71	33.35	8.68	3.71	19.28	24.63	5.34
	Total	18.8	18.5	11.62	5.97	45.25	53.9	8.72

Source: Tables of Agricultural Statistics of Sawai Madhopur District, 1975-76.

APPENDIX XI

Area Classification (Percentage in Geographical Area 1985-86)

Sl. No.	Name of the Tahsil	Forest	Not available for cultivation	Other un-cultivated land excluding follow land	Fallow land	Net area sown	Total cropped area	Area sown more than once
1.	Sawai Madhopur	19.69%	17.2%	6.50	8.02	48.63	51.21	2.25
2.	Khandar	34.79	13.9	13.85	3.43	34.00	35.41	1.04
3.	Boanli	3.57	17.24	9.90	13.59	56.10	63.0	6.60
4.	Gangapur	3.25	11.93	9.6	9.30	64.61	78.18	12.09
5.	Bamanwas	5.40	14.32	9.86	7.3	63.5	67.56	4.72
6.	Nadoti	14.08	10.30	5.35	4.6	66.15	72.30	2.73
7.	Hindaun	2.34	16.09	14.06	5.00	62.5	92.62	28.00
8.	Todabhim	5.13	11.92	7.96	5.55	70.37	92.59	22.2
9.	Mahuwa	2.6	11.50	5.41	6.25	75.0	98.00	23.33
10.	Karauli	40.60	20.43	12.66	4.34	22.1	28.9	6.66
11.	Sapotra	52.1	16.78	7.5	3.57	20.71	25.85	10.50
	Total	22.47	15.84	9.43	6.22	46.00	54.26	8.27

Source: Tables of Agricultural Statistics of Sawai Madhopur District, 1985-86.

APPENDIX XII

Decadal Variation (1975-76 to 1985-86) of Land Utilisation (% hectares)

Sl. No.	Name of the Tahsil	Forest	Not available for cultivation	Other un-cultivated (excluding) Fallow land	Fallow land	Net area sown	Total cropped area	Area sown more than once
1.	Sawai Madhopur	-1.16 (D)	+2.74 (A)	-2.83 (D)	+2.37 (A)	-0.97 (D)	-0.25 (D)	+0.47 (A)
2.	Khandar	+6.67 (A)	-3.07 (D)	-5.21 (D)	-0.84 (D)	+2.21	+3.12 (A)	+0.57 (A)
3.	Boanli	+1.02 (B)	+1.04 (A)	-2.4 (D)	+2.67 (A)	-1.84 (D)	+0.51 (A)	+2.1 (A)
4.	Gangapur	3.25 (C)	+2.79 (A)	-4 (A)	-0.46 (D)	+0.35 (B)	+2.37 (A)	+0.61 (A)
5.	Bamanwas	+0.68 (B)	+0.82 (A)	-2.3 (D)	+0.14 (B)	1.00 (A)	-4.73 (D)	-5.01 (D)
6.	Nadoti	+0.92 (B)	-1.04 (B)	-1.84 (B)	-2.49 (D)	+4.82 (A)	-1.55 (A)	-6.64 (D)
7.	Hindaun	2.34 (C)	-0.8 (B)	-0.74 (B)	+0.64 (A)	+0.79 (A)	+1.83 (A)	-0.24 (B)
8.	Todabhim	+1.83 (B)	-0.48 (B)	-3.04 (D)	-0.32 (D)	+2.57 (A)	-6.83 (D)	-3.11 (D)
9.	Mahuwa	+0.51 (B)	+0.21 (A)	-1.07 (B)	+0.43 (A)	+0.53 (B)	-7.8 (D)	-2.29 (D)
10.	Karauli	+3.8 (A)	-3.74 (D) (D) (D)	-0.16 (B)	-0.34 (D)	+0.55 (B)	+2.8 (A)	+0.59 (A)
11.	Sapotra	+16.39 (A)	-16.57 (D)	-1.18 (B)	-0.14 (D)	+1.43 (B)	+1.22 (A)	+5.16 (A)
	District Average	+3.7	-2.48	-2.19	+0.25	+0.75	+0.36	-0.45

Index: A = More than average from the District average ± geographical area; B = Less than average; C = Constant; D = Declire.

Source: Tables of Agricultural Statistics of Sawai Madhopur District, 1975-76 to 1985-86.

BIBLIOGRAPHY

Abrahams, A.D. (1972), "Drainage densities and sediment yields in Eastern Australia". *Australian Geographical Studies*, Vol 1, pp.19-41.

Ahmad, E. (1968), "Distribution and causes of gully erosion in India." *Selected Papers*, Vol 1; 21st International Geographical Congress, p.2.

——— (1973), *Soil erosion in India.* Asia Publishing House, Calcutta, pp.63-64.

Ali, M. (1974), "Halt and menace of slopy lands." *Indian Farmers Digest*, 7(9), pp.31-34.

Allen, J.P.L. (1965), *A review of the original characteristics of recent alluvial sediments.* Sedimentology, 5:2.

Allen, P.A. (1985), *Sedimentary structure, their character and physical basin.* 1-Elsvier, Amsterdam.

Amalkar and Bandyopadhyay, (1974), "Mechanism of Rills : An investigation in Micro-geomorphology." *Geographical Review of India*, Vol 36, No 3, pp.31-38.

Amani, K.Z., (1970), "Geography and Landuse planning." *Philippine Geographical Journal* (Manila), Vol 14, p.46.

Antevs, E.V. (1952), "Arroyo-cutting and filling." *Journal of Geol.* Vol 60, pp.375-385.

Asthana, V.K., (1967), "Morphometric evaluation of landforms of Almora and its environs." *National Geographical Journal*, India, Vol 13, pp.37-45.

Babu, P.V.L.P., (1978), "Geomorphology of Krishna Godavari Delta region – Interpretation from Landsat Imagery." *National Geographical Journal*, India, Vol 24, pp.55-61.

Babu, R., Tejwani, C.G., Aggarwal, H.C. (1978), "Distribution of erosion index and iso-erodent map of India." *Indian Journal of Soil Conservation*, 6(1), pp.1-12.

Balak, R. and Joshi, D.C. (1984), Landuse soil relationship in an Arid Zone Area." *The Deccan Geographer*, Vol XXII, No 1 & 2, p.505.

Bali, J.S. (1972a), *Report of Working Group on Ravine Reclamation Programme for the Dacoit Infested Area of UP, MP and Rajasthan.* Government of India, Ministry of Home Affairs, New Delhi.

—— (1972b), "Criteria for landuse planning in the Ravines." Proc. Symp. on Reclamation and Use of Wastelands in India, *Bulletin of the Indian National Science Academy*, 40, pp.170-174.

—— (1972c), "New trends in ravine control and reclamation", Proc. Symp. on Reclamation and Use of Wastelands in India, *Bulletin of the Indian National Science Academy*, 40, pp.162-169.

Balmiki, P. G.S.I., (1984), *Geology, sedimentation and paleo—geography of the Vindhyan Super Group*, South Eastern Rajasthan.

Banerji, B., (1985), "Genesis of floods in West Bengal and their impact on Society", *The Deccan Geographer*, Vol. XXIII, No 1, p.40.

Banerji, A.K. and Sinha, P.M. (1976), *Structure and tectonics of Vindhyan in eastern Rajasthan.* Symposium on Vindhyan Central India, Bhopal, Abstract.

Bennett, H.H. (1939)., Soil conservation, McGraw-Hill Book Company, New York, p.513.

Beyer, J.L., (1974), Global response to natural hazards floods. In *National Hazards*, ed. G.F. White, New York, Oxford University Press, pp.265-74.

Bhattacharya, A., (1983), "Geologic and geomorphic controls in landuse pattern – Example using remote sensing technique". *Photonirvachak*, Vol 11, No 3, pp.57-64.

Bhimaya, C.P. and Kaul, R.N. (1960), "Some afforestation problems and research needs in relation to erosion control in arid and semi-arid parts of Rajasthan." *Indian Forester*, 86, pp.453-468.

Bogolyubova, I.V. and Karaushev, A.V., (1979), "*Problem of gully formation and development*, Soviet Hydrology." Selected Papers, 18, pp.225-264.

Bryan, K., (1925), "Date of channel trenching (arroyo-cutting) in the Arid South-West." *Science*, 62, pp.338-344.

Buckman, H.O. and Brady, N.C., (1971), *The Nature and Properties of soils.* Macmillan, New York.

Carson, M.A. and S.W. Tan, (1981), "The land conservation conundrum of Eastern Barbados." *Annals of the Assoc. of Am. Geogs*, Vol 67, pp.185-203.

Chakraborty, B.C. and Ghosh, (1974), "Longitudinal profiles in fluvial process." *Geographical Review of India*, Vol 36, pp.1-5.

Chandrabhan, (1977), "Geomorphology of Agra district, Micro morphogenetic analysis." *Geographical Review of India*, Vol 39(1), pp.71-75.

Chatterjee, S.P. and Bagchi, K., (1957) "Geomorphic Regions of Eastern Rajasthan Pathar." *Geographical Review of India*, Vol 19, No 4, pp.42-47.

Chorley, R.J., (1971), *The drainage basin as the fundamental geomorphic unit. An Introduction of Physical Hydrology*, (R.J. Chorley, ed.) London, pp.37-59.

Coulson, A.L., (1927), "Geology of Bundi state Rajasthan", *Rec. Geological Survey*, India, Vol 50, pp.185-199.

Cooke, R.U., (1974), "The rainfall extent of arroyo imitation in southern Arizons." *Zeitschrift fur Geomorphologie supple.*, 21, pp.63-75.

Cooke, R.U. and Reeves, R.W., (1976), "*Arroyos and environmental change in the American South West.*" Oxford Research Studies in Geography, Clarendon Press, Oxford.

Dayal, R.C., (1975), *Halt the march of ravines*. Intensive Agriculture, 13(4), p.20.

De, N.K., (1982), "Land Classification: A study in applied geomorphology" in *Perspective of Geomorphology* (Ed.), by H.S. Sharma, Vol III, pp.179-190.

Denevan, W.M., (1967), "Livestock number in 19th Century New Mexico and the problem of gullying in the south west." *Annals of the Assoc. of Am. Geogs*, 57, pp.691-703.

Desai M., (1976), "A brief geomorphological account of the south Koel Basin". *Geographical Review*, India, Vol 38, pp 374-381.

Dhurvanarayan, V.V. and Babu, R., (1983), "Estimation of soil erosion in India." American Society of Civil Engineers, *Journal of the Irrigation and Drainage Division*, 109, pp.419-436.

Digar, S., et al., (1974), "Symposium soil genesis, classification and land management." *Indian Society of Social Sciences*, Calcutta.

Dillon, S.S., (1977), "The impact of landforms on Agricultural landuse in Manasu District (Himachal Pradesh)." *Geographical Review of India*, Vol 39, 2, June, p.183.

Dokuchaev, V.V. (1951), "Soil classification." (Northern Hemisphere – *Natural Soil Zones, 1900*). Vol VI, Science Academy, USSR.

Edward, A.K., (1979), *Environmental Geology*. Second edition, University of California, Santa Barbara.

Enadu, S.N., (1981), *Flood problems in Ilorin*. Unpublished B.Sc. dissertation, p.68, Department of Geog. University of Ilorin.

Ganpati, S. and Srinivasan, S., (1979), "A reinterpretation of architecture of the Great Boundary Fault with special reference to Chittorgarh Area." Rajasthan, India.

Gardiner, V.C., (1981), "The impact of climate on fluvial system." *Perspectives in Geomorphology* (Ed.), H.S. Sharma, Vol. III Concept Publishing Company, New Delhi.

Gautam, N.C. and Narayan, L.R.A., (1982), *Suggested National Landuse land cover classification system for India using Remote Sensing Techniques*. Pink Publishing House, Mathura.

Gawande, S.P., Shanwara, P.G. and Joshi, O.P., (1980), "Characterisation and management of salt affected ravinous soil of Sultanpur block." Kota, Rajasthan, India, *Journal of Soil Conservation* 8(1), pp.8-14.

Gellert, J.F., 1982, "Principles of geomorphological regionalization and encoding of geomorphological characteristics for computer processing of data." In *Perspectives in Geomorphology*, (Ed.), H.S. Sharma, Vol III, pp.237-242.

Geological Survey of India, Memoirs, Vol 116 (Part I and II).

Ghosh, B. and Singh, S., (1985), "Observation on geomorphology and landuse of a Kitnod village." *Geographical Review*, India, Vol 27, pp.144-156.

Ghosh, D.K., (1982), "Geomorphology of Ravi Basin in NW Himachal Himalaya and Environmental Management." In *Perspectives in Geomorphology*, (Ed.) H.S. Sharma, Vol III, pp.53-83.

Ghosh, D., and Chhibar, I.B., (1984), "Aid to photo-interpretation in the identification of geomorphic and geological feature around Chamba-Dharamshala Area, HP." *Photonirvachak*, Vol 12, No 1, pp.55-62.

Gidwani, H.M., Aggrawal, M.C. and Dubey, L.N., (1967), "Crop rotation for reclaimed ravine lands." *Journal of Soil and Water Conservation in India*, 15(1, 2).

Goswami, A. and Das, A.L., (1984), "Impact of landscape on soils – A case study of Bankura (W. Bengal)." *Geographical Review of India*, Vol 46, No 1, March, pp.139-147.

Government of India, (1907), *Soil Survey Manual of the All India Soil and Landuse Survey Organisation*. IARI, New Delhi.

Government of India's Planning Commission, (1965), *Study on survey and reclamation of Ravines in India*. Delhi.

Government of Rajasthan, (1981), Department of Agriculture, *Report on Soil Survey and Land Classification of Panchna Irrigation Project* (Sawai Madhopur). Soil Survey Organisation, Rajasthan, Jaipur.

Government of Rajasthan, (1981), *Sawai Madhopur District Gazetteer*.

Govindrajan, S.V., (1972), "Wastelands and their better use through soil surveys." *Bulletin of Indian National Science Academy*, p.44.

Gupta, R.K., (1973), "Publication Corner: Annotated bibliography on ravine lands." *Soil Conservation Digest*, 2(1), pp.88-94.

Gupta, R.K. and Prajapati, M.C., (1983), *Reclamation and use of ravine lands*. Desert Resources and Technology (Jodhpur) 1, pp.221-262.

Hackett, C.A., (1881), "Geology of Aravalli Region Central and Eastern," *Reclamation Geological Survey of India*, Vol. 19, p.4.

Heron, A.M., (1917), "Geology of north-eastern Rajputana and adjacent districts." *Memoir Geological Survey of India*, XLV, Pt 1.

—, (1938), "The Gwalior and Vindhyan systems of south eastern Rajputana." *Memoirs Geological Survey of India*, Vol 45, Part D, pp.127-179.

Horton, R., (1945). "Erosional development of streams and their drainage basins." *Bulletin Geological Society of America*, 56, pp.275-370.

Hudson, N.W., (1983), "Soil conservation strategies in the third world." *Journal of Soil Conservation*, 38, pp.446-450.

Hussain, M., (1963), *Land utilization in the upper Ganga Yamuna Doab*. Ph.D. Thesis, Aligarh Muslim University.

Icballudin *et al*., (1976), "Genesis of the Great Boundary Fault of Rajasthan, India." *Proceedings of the third Regional Conference on Geology and Mineral Resources of Southeast Asia*, Bangkok, pp.14-18.

Iyer, H.S. and Srinivasan, T.R., (1977), "Land resources inventories, for integrated landuse planning with special reference to catchment of Pohru river in J & K. State." *Photonirvachak*, V. 5(2), pp.71-80.

Jose, C.S. *et al*., (1981), "Runoff/Watersheds," *Indian Journal of Soil Conservation*, Vol 9, pp.33-42.

Karanth, K.R., (1980), *Bulletin of GSI*, Series B, Engineering Geology and Groundwater No.32. "Geology and Ground Water Resources of Upper Luni-Basin, Ajmer District, Rajasthan."

Kaushik, S.D., (1965), "Geomorphology of Rejuvenation in the Garhwal Himalaya." *Indian Geographical Journal*, Vol 40, No 1, and 2, pp.13-19.

Kawamoto, C. *et al.*, (1980), "Study on the flood caused by heavy rainfall on Aug 4-7, 1979 in Kitakawi river basin." *Annals of the Tohuku Geographical Association*, Vol. 32, pp.127-137.

Kayastha, S.L., (1975), "Some aspects of soil erosion and conservation in India." *National Geographical Journal of India*, 11(1).

Kharakwal, S.C., (1971), "Slope studies on the Himalayan Terrain," *The National Geographical Journal of India*, Vol 3, Pt 1, p.1.

Khybri, M.L., (1973), "Ravine reclamation in Kota." *Soil Conservation Digest*, 3, pp.57-60.

Klimaszewski, M., (1963), *Problems of geomorphological mapping, Warszawa.* Inst. of Geog., Polish Academy of Sciences, Warszawa, pp.67-71, 95-98, 121-126.

Koppen, W. Geiger, R., (1954), *Klimader Erde (Map), Justus Perthes, Darmotadt*, Germany. American Distributor, A.J. Nystrom and Company, Chicago.

Krishnan, M.S. and Swaminath, J., (1959), "The Great Vindhyan Basin of Northern India." *Journal Geographical Society of India*, V 1, pp.10-30.

Krishnan, M.S., (1968), "*Geology of India and Burma.*" 5th Edn., Higginbathama, Madras.

Leopold, L.B., Walman, M.G. and Miller, J.P., (1964), *Fluvial processes in geomorphology*. San Francisco, W.H. Freeman.

Martin, J.H., (1984), "Ravine erosion and reclamation in India," *Geoform*, Vol 15, No 4, pp. 543-561.

Mathur, C.M., Ganu, S.N. and Jain, S.V., (1975), "Soils of Rajasthan, Survey and Classification in Retrospect and Prospects." *Soil Survey Organization*, Department of Agriculture, Rajasthan, Jaipur.

Medicott, H.B., (1868), "The boundary of Vindhyan Series in Rajputana." *Rec, GSI*, V 1, Pt 3.

Milap, C., (1986), "*Regional geomorphology of Lahaul* (Central Himalaya)." Unpublished M. Phil dissertation Centre for the study of Regional Development, JNU, New Delhi.

Mukhopadhyay, S.C., (1979), "The morphological analysis of landforms of the Tista Basin in the Eastern Himalaya, India." *Geographical Review of India*, Vol 41, No 4, pp.347-356.

Narain, P., Verma, B. and Singha, A.K., (1979), "Studies of soils of Chambal with regard to their erodibility." *Indian Journal of Soil Conservation*, 7(2), pp 37-42.

Narain, P., Patel, A.P., (1975), "*Annual Progress Report.*" Central Soil and Water Conservation Research Institute, Kota.

Natarajan, S., Gajbe, M.Y. and Manchanda, M.L., (1986), "Landuse study in Mewat Area, Haryana." *Photonirvachak, Journal of the Indian Society of Remote Sensing*, Vol 14, No 1.

Negi, B.S., (1978), "Soil types, fertility and landuse in Garhwal district." *Geographical Review of India*, No 3, pp. 256.

Nigam, R., Lodha, B.K. and Seth, S.P., *Report on soil fertility status of Sawai Madhopur district.* Office of the Soil Survey Officer, Durgapura, Jaipur (Rajasthan).

Nookaraju, D. and Vaidyanadhan, R., (1971), "Hill slope elements surfacial deposits near Visakhapatnam, Andhra Pradesh." *Journal of the Indian Geoscience Association*, Vol 13, pp.45-51.

Olaniron, O.J. Dr., (1983), "Flood generating mechanisms at Iorin, Nigeria," *Geojournal* 7-3, pp.271-277.

Oya, M., (1980), "Multifunctional uses of geomorphological survey maps in identifying flood stricken areas and land types." *National Geographer*, Vol XV, No 2, p.173.

Padmaja, G., (1976), "Geomorphology of the Mej Basin (Rajasthan)" unpublished Ph.D. Thesis, University of Rajasthan.

Pandey, S., Ghosh, B. and Roy, B.S., (1967), "Geomorphic influence and soil genesis in semi-arid environment." *Journal of Indian Society of Social Sciences*, 15, p.163.

Pareek, B.L. and Seth, S.P., (1970), "Soils of Rajasthan." *Fertilizer Association of India*, 15, p.62.

Parthasarthy, Y.J. and Vaidyanadhan, R., (1976), "Pediments and pediment forming processes around Coimbatore, South India." *The Indian Geographical Society Golden Jubilee* Vol V 50, pp.252-259.

Pascoe, S.E.H., "*A Manual of the Geology of India and Burma.*" Vol I and II.

Petit, M. and Bourgeat, F., (1965), "Les Lavaka Malgaches: Un agent natural d' evolution des versants." *Bulletin de l' Assoc. de Geogs.*, Francais, 332/333, pp.29-33.

Pofali, R.M. and Sita Ram, (1985), "Importance of Remote Sensing Technique for Geomorphic Mapping – A Case Study of Western Ghats (Maharashtra)." *The Deccan Geographer*, Vol 22, No 2 & 3, pp.105-114.

Prajapati, M.C., Joshie, P., Rathore, B.L. and Dubey, L.N. (1982), "Surface water management for grass and tree-land development in ravinous watershed. A Case Study," *Indian Journal of Soil Conservation* 10(2/3), 30-80.

Prandini, F.L., (1974), "Occurrence of 'Bocorocas' in S. Brazil." *International Assoc of Engineering, Geology, Proceeding*, 1(3), pp.36.1 to 36.10.

Raghavswamy, V. and Vaidyanadhan, R., (1980), "Morphology and Land systems of a part of Visakhapatnam A.P." Photonirvachak, *Journal Indian Society Photo Interpretation, Remote Sensing*, Vol 8, No 1, 1980, pp.9-21.

Rai, R.K., (1980), "*Geomorphology of the Sonar Berma Basin*, M.P." Concept Publishing Company, New Delhi.

———, Patnaik, S.N., Panda, P. and Singhavi, V., (1981), "Hill slopes, landuse and soil erosion around Shillong (Meghalaya)." *Geographical Review of India.*

——— and Pramila, K., (1972). "Has Deccan foreland rejuvenated?" *The Geographer*, 19, pp. 34-36.

Raju, P.K.N. and Vaidyanadhan, R., (1977), "Study of landforms, landuse and land units of a part of Krishna District, A.P. from Aerial Photographs." *Photonirvachak*, Vol 5, No 2, pp.41-46.

Ranbir, S., (1967), "Rajasthan enact a Soil Conservation Legislation." *Journal of Soil and Water Conservation in India*, 15(3, 4).

Reddy, N.B.K. and Reddy, D.N. (1981). "Agriculture in Arid and semi-arid regions of India." *Trans. Institute of Indian Geographers*, Vol. 3, (2), pp. 127-31.

Rodha, J.C. (1969), *The flood hydrography in earth, water and man.* Chorley (ed.), pp.405-418, Methuen & Co Ltd London.

Rostvedt, J.C. *et al.* (1968), "Summary of floods in the United States during 1963." *US Geog Surv. Wat. Sup.*, Pap. 1839-B.

Roy, B.B. and Sen, A.K., (1968), "Social map of Rajasthan." *Annals of Arid Zone*, 7, pp.1-14.

Roy, B.S., (1982), "The Economic Geology and Mineral Resources of Rajasthan and Ajmer." *Memoirs of the Geological Survey of India*, Vol 86.

Roy, B.K., (1968), "Measurement of Rural landuse in Azamgarh." *The Geographer*, Vol XI; pp.78-100.

Saminathan, R., (1985), "Towards a flood control policy." *The Geography Teacher India*, Vol 20, Nos 1-3.

Subramanyam, V., (1986), "Analysis and interpretation of the topographical map." DST Winter School, Geomorphology, 1-12 Dec 1986, pp.3, Department Earth Sciences, IIT, Bombay.

Subramanyam, V., (1986), "Application of fluvial Geomorphology." pp.21.1, DST Winter School for Young Scientists in *Geomorphology*, 1-12 Dec 1986, Department Earth Sciences, IIT, Bombay.

Subramanyam, V., (1978), "Landsystem studies for resources evaluation – A demonstration around Sagar, M.P." *Photonirvachak*, Vol. 6(1), pp.31-42.

Subramanyan, V., (1986), "Geomorphic application in Pedo-ecological Surveys. pp.22.1, DST Winter School for Young Scientists in Geomorphology, 1-12 Dec 1986, Department of Earth Sciences, IIT, Bombay.

Takenchi, K., (1950), "Study on the Flooding of the Iwai River caused by Son Typhoon on September 23, 1948." *Annals of the Tokuku Geographical Association*, Vol 4, Nos 3 & 4, pp.35-37.

Tawde, M.D., (1978), "Geomorphic studies and Agricultural landuse planning." *National Geographer*, Vol XIII(1), pp.75-82.

Twidale, C.R., (1960), "Some problems of slope development." *Journal of Geographic Society of Australia* V 6, pp.131-148.

Tejwani, K.J., (1972), "Classification and reclamation of ravine lands." *Bulletin of Indian National Sciences Academy*, 44.

Tejwani, K.G. Dharma, V.V. and Satyanarain, T., (1960), "Control of gully erosion in the ravine lands of Gujarat." *Journal of Soil and Water Conservation in India*, Vol 8, No 1, p.65.

Tricart, J., (1972), "*Landforms of humid tropics, forests and Savannans*." Longmans, London.

Uchida, M.O., (1986), "Relationship between geomorphology and flooding in the Ichioscki Plain of the Kitakawai river basin, Japan." *National Geographer*, Vol XXI, No 1, pp.33-49.

USDA (1978), "Soil texonomy agriculture handbook." No 436, *Soil Conservation Service*, Washington, D.C. (USA).

Vasantha, K.T., (1985), "Floods in Tamil Nadu: Causes and Control." *The Geography Teacher, India*, Vol 20, Nos 1-3.

Vats, P.C., (1983), "Geomorphic factors in landuse planning – A case study of village Asan Tiloria." *The Geographical Observer*, Vol 19, pp.11-16.

Vats, P.C., (1986), "Geomorphological factors affecting land utilization in Pali district. Western Rajasthan." *The Geographical Observer*, Vol 21, pp.37-46.

Vats, P.C., (1987), "Application of Remote Sensing Techniques in Geomorphological Investigation – A case study of Pali district, Western Rajasthan." *The Deccan Geographer*, Vol XXV, p.139.

Verma, B., (1981), *Classification of ravines for optimum utilization in India*. Central Soil and Water Conservation Research Centre, Kota.

Verma, R.P., (1981), *A decade of environmental geoscientific studies by Geological Survey of India*. Special Publication Series No 9, pp.61-64.

Verma, R.P., and Roy, P.K., (1981), "Palaeo-drainage studies and its utility in flood problems – A case history in Lower Luni Basin." *Perspectives in Geomorphology*, Vol IV, pp.137-143.

Vithal, M.K.P.R., and Rao, U., (1980)," The determination of Assured Precipitation etc." *The Deccan Geographer*, Vol XVIII, pp.788-793.

Wadia, D.N., (1938), "The structure of the Himalayas and of North India Poreland." *Proceedings Indian Science Congress*, 25, pp.91-118.

Yadav, B.R. and Gupta, R.N., (1974), "A comparative study of clay minerology of semi-arid soils of western U.P. and eastern Rajasthan." *Proceedings of the Indian National Academy of Science*, Part B, 40(2).

Yadav, U.K., (1961), "Role of rain drops in soil erosion." *Journal of Soil and Water Conservation in India*, Vol 9, Nos 3 & 4, p.180.

Young, A., (1972), "*Slopes*." Edinberg: Oliver and Boyd, pp.250-252.

Zarkragewska, B., (1963), "An analysis of landforms in a part of the Central Great Plains." *Annals of the Association of American Geography*, Vol 53, No 4, pp.536-568.